SUPERIOR DONUTS

BY TRACY LETTS

★

★

DRAMATISTS
PLAY SERVICE
INC.

SUPERIOR DONUTS
Copyright © 2010, Tracy Letts

All Rights Reserved

SPECIAL NOTE

SPECIAL NOTE ON SONGS AND RECORDINGS

For Mom

ACKNOWLEDGMENTS

Tina Landau.

Martha Lavey, David Hawkanson, Erica Daniels, Amy Morton, Steppenwolf Theatre Company.

Jeffrey Richards, Jean Doumanian, Jerry Frankel.

Jane Alderman, Kate Buddeke, Cliff Chamberlain, Michael Garvey, Jon Michael Hill, Robert Maffia, Michael McKean, James Vincent Meredith, Yasen Peyankov.

Ed Sobel, James Schuette, Loy Arcenas, Chris Akerlind, Ana Kuzmanic, Michael Bodeen, Rob Milburn, Rick Sordelet, Chuck Coyl, Artie Gaffin, Laura D. Glenn, Lauren Hickman.

Ron Gwiazda, Amy Wagner.

Nicole Wiesner.

The fam.

SUPERIOR DONUTS received its world premiere at Steppenwolf Theatre in Chicago, Illinois, in June 2008. It was directed by Tina Landau; the set design was by Loy Arcenas; the costume design was by Ana Kuzmanic; the lighting design was by Christopher Akerlind; the sound design was by Michael Bodeen and Rob Milburn; the fight direction was by Chuck Coyl; and the stage manager was Laura D. Glenn. The cast was as follows:

MAX TARASOV	Yasen Peyankov
OFFICER RANDY OSTEEN	Kate Buddeke
OFFICER JAMES BAILEY	James Vincent Meredith
LADY BOYLE	Jane Alderman
ARTHUR PRZYBYSZEWSKI	Michael McKean
FRANCO WICKS	Jon Michael Hill
LUTHER FLYNN	Robert Maffia
KEVIN MAGEE	Cliff Chamberlain
KIRIL IVAKIN	Michael Garvey

The Steppenwolf production of SUPERIOR DONUTS received its Broadway premiere at the Music Box Theatre on October 1, 2009. It was directed by Tina Landau; the set design was by James Schuette; the costume design was by Ana Kuzmanic; the lighting design was by Christopher Akerlind; the sound design was by Rob Milburn and Michael Bodeen; the hair and wig design were by Charles LaPointe; the dramaturgy was by Edward Sobel; the fight direction was by Rick Sordelet; and the production stage manager was Arthur Gaffin. The cast was as follows:

MAX TARASOV	Yasen Peyankov
OFFICER RANDY OSTEEN	Kate Buddeke
OFFICER JAMES BAILEY	James Vincent Meredith
LADY BOYLE	Jane Alderman
ARTHUR PRZYBYSZEWSKI	Michael McKean
FRANCO WICKS	Jon Michael Hill
LUTHER FLYNN	Robert Maffia
KEVIN MAGEE	Cliff Chamberlain
KIRIL IVAKIN	Michael Garvey

CHARACTERS
(in order of appearance)

MAX TARASOV, 49 years old, Russian

OFFICER RANDY OSTEEN, 49 years old, Irish-American

OFFICER JAMES BAILEY, 43 years old, African-American

LADY BOYLE, 72 years old, Irish-American

ARTHUR PRZYBYSZEWSKI ("[p]Shub-er-shef-ski"), 59 years old, Polish-American

FRANCO WICKS, 21 years old, African-American

LUTHER FLYNN, 45 years old, Irish/Italian-American

KEVIN MAGEE, 28 years old, Irish-American

KIRIL IVAKIN, 35 years old, Russian

PLACE

Superior Donuts, a small donut shop
in Chicago's Uptown neighborhood.

TIME

December 2009–January 2010.

So in the dark we hide the heart that bleeds,
And wait, and tend our agonizing seeds.

—Countee Cullen

SUPERIOR DONUTS

ACT ONE

At rise:

The donut shop.

The glass front door and display case have been shattered. One wall has been spray painted with a single word: PUSSY.

Randy (female), a uniformed cop, listens to Max and fills out paperwork. James, another uniformed cop, walks around the store, inspects the graffiti, surveys the damage.

MAX. A real fucking shame, y'know? Little son-of-a-bitches trash *my* store too, just next door, twice in three years. Now I got more locks than they got in White House, and so they come torture *this* poor man. Why they do this to this man? Must we all live behind bars?

RANDY. I want to hear all this, Max, but let's start with your name.

MAX. You *know* my name. You just now *say* my name.

RANDY. Your *full* name. Your *last* name —

MAX. I am not the person who has done this, this is not my store, I do not know why my name is all so important as —

JAMES. Answer the question. *(Lady Boyle, an elderly homeless woman, enters. James deals with her.)*

RANDY. You made the call. I just need it for my report.

LADY. What happened?

MAX. Max Tarasov.

JAMES. Nothing, Lady, you got to move on —

RANDY. Oops, all right, spell that.

LADY. Where's Arthur? Is Arthur okay?

9

MAX. M-A-X T-A-R-A-S-O-V.

RANDY. Like it sounds.

MAX. Like it sound, yes.

RANDY. And you run the video store next door.

MAX. How many times you come in my store?

RANDY. C'mon.

JAMES. Arthur's okay, but you got to move on.

LADY. Can I get a donut?

JAMES. Come back later for your donut, but for now —

LADY. You want me to go.

JAMES. Yes, ma'am.

LADY. I'm goin'. *(Lady exits.)*

MAX. Uptown International DVD Rental, right next door, ten-nineteen. You want me to spell DVD?

RANDY. And you think you know who did this?

MAX. I see the little black son-of-a-bitches every day, no offense. They run in my store smelling like the pot. They are ripping off my DVDs, they break in my store and write their paints on my walls, twice in three years. Have you not heard me or not?

JAMES. Calm down.

MAX. Is anyone paying attention in America? Our neighborhood needs help. They put in Starbuck and you think they do not sell drugs on corner still? What, you think Starbuck stop drugs? These black son-of-a-bitches don't care about Starbuck. No offense.

JAMES. These guys you say did this, you can name them?

MAX. I do not know names, but come back tonight and I will point them out to you. James, you know who they are! They are same ones who do all crime on this street!

JAMES. How is it a man who runs a DVD store shows up to his place of work before a man who sells donuts?

MAX. I do not —

JAMES. Lot of people anxious to rent DVDs at six in the morning?

MAX. I do not "run" DVD store. I own DVD store; I am the pro-prietor. 'Kay? I am here early because I expanse my store and a lot of work needs to be done. I have three workers here from Nizhny, just arrived, do not speak the language, and they have red necks, so I will not allow them to work unsupervise. I see Arthur's shop is smashed and so I call you police because I am a good citizen. I am guilty of nothing other than working hard. I am guilty only of living American dream. And why Arthur is not here is not my business. Some day Arthur does not show up at all. Why he treat his shop in such lazy fashion is not for me to say.

RANDY. Arthur's been closed a lot lately.

MAX. You know his wife die.

RANDY. Arthur's not married.

MAX. No. Yes. His former wife.

RANDY. He's *not* married.

MAX. Not now. She's dead.

RANDY. But he was married before she died.

MAX. He was married, then he was divorced, then she die.

JAMES. How'd she die?

MAX. He does not tell me these things. I find that out from douchebag who work here some days, that Ray. But no, since she die, Arthur has not been so much on his balls.

JAMES. "On the ball."

MAX. Yes, not so much.

RANDY. He doesn't talk to you?

MAX. We talk every day. "Hello, how are you, can I have a donut." I know Arthur eleven years, since I first come to America, since I open my store. All my life I try to buy his shop from him but he will not sell. I give him good price, is very frustrating. But Arthur always help me when I ask, help me with language and give me free everything. But he is private man. He is not natural ... no, how do you say this? He is not in nature a man who wants to talk.

RANDY. It's not in his nature.

MAX. Yes. Thank you. It is not in his nature. He is a good man, Arthur, I think, and I call him my friend, but no, he does not want to be pulled into light, so I do not pull. (*Arthur enters. His clothes are unwashed, wrinkled; his hair is a greasy gray tangle tied in a pony-tail; he sports a scraggly beard; he is half asleep, maybe stoned; he is a mess. No one speaks as he surveys the damage.*)

ARTHUR. I'll make some coffee.

MAX. It's a goddamn fucking shame, Arthur.

ARTHUR. Yeah ...

MAX. A goddamn fucking shame.

ARTHUR. Anybody want coffee? Randy? Coffee?

RANDY. Yes.   JAMES. Yeah.

MAX. Please, coffee. Arthur. I show up this morning and see your store is smashed so I call police. I hope you don't mind.

ARTHUR. What day is it?

RANDY. Tuesday.

ARTHUR. You sure?

11

RANDY. Yeah.

ARTHUR. My coffee guy comes Mondays. Sure it's not Monday?

MAX. Monday was yesterday, Arthur. You were not here yesterday.

ARTHUR. I think I missed my coffee guy. *(Beat.)* I missed my coffee guy. *(Beat.)* I don't have any coffee. *(Digs for wallet.)* Anybody want Starbucks?

JAMES. Arthur, who did this to your store?

ARTHUR. I don't know.

JAMES. Got a theory?

ARTHUR. No.

MAX. I have theory, if anyone is interested. Little black son-of-a-bitches sell drugs on corner smash up. How is that for theory? Arthur, you know this is true.

ARTHUR. I'm going to Starbucks.

MAX. I am more angry than he is. They smash *his* store, and I am more angry than he is. Why are you not angry?

ARTHUR. I just need coffee.

MAX. Then maybe you get angry *later* when those black son-of-a-bitches on the corner laugh at you, call you "old hippie" —

JAMES. Thank you for your information. Thank you for making the call. You are free to go.

MAX. I am?

JAMES. You should go. Now.

MAX. I cannot say they are black? Have I done something wrong?

JAMES. I'm not *asking* you —

MAX. You are black man, I see this. I do not say you do crime. I do not say *you* are black son-of-a-bitch. Am I not allowed to call black people, "black people"?

JAMES. *(Nose to nose with Max.)* Say one more word about black people and I'm gonna bust your lip.

MAX. *(Quietly, to Arthur.)* I come by later.

ARTHUR. Mm. Thanks for calling, the um … thanks. *(Max glares at James, backs to door …)*

MAX. So much for my inalienable rights! *(… And quickly exits.)*

JAMES. *Russians*, y'know? Russians and Polacks.

RANDY. I wish I could tell you there's something we could do, but truth is. I mean if we happen to pick somebody up and they tell us something, but that's not likely.

JAMES. Max is wrong, you know, this isn't Up-Town Lawds. They'd hit it with a CVL tag, bunny or five-pointed star. And they would've boosted some shit too, at least the register. This is just random, or somebody hates you.

ARTHUR. Hate crime.

JAMES. No, hate crime's aimed at specific social groups, minorities.

RANDY. Pussies aren't a social group.

JAMES. You got insurance, right?

ARTHUR. Well, I'll ... see what it covers, but yeah.

RANDY. You better call a board-up service.

ARTHUR. Uh-huh. Yeah.

JAMES. Sorry, Arthur.

ARTHUR. Yeah, what a drag.

JAMES. I feel bad, you know? I mean we're in here —

RANDY. — Yeah, we're in here a *lot* —

JAMES. Maybe you need more security.

ARTHUR. Interesting concept.

RANDY. Where's what's-his-name? Douchebag works here some days. What's his name?

ARTHUR. Ray. Ray Klapprott.

JAMES. Pretty name.

ARTHUR. He moved on.

RANDY. What for?

ARTHUR. I don't recall ...

JAMES. All right.

ARTHUR. I'm sorry.

JAMES. For what.

ARTHUR. I don't know.

RANDY. You wouldn't want to go get us some coffee, would you?

JAMES. Yeah, sure. Arthur, you want coffee?

ARTHUR. *(Fishing for money.)* Oh, please.

JAMES. No, I got it. I need some cigs, too. You need cigs, Randy?

RANDY. Yeah, thanks. *(James exits. Arthur draws shades over windows.)* Closing up shop.

ARTHUR. Just till I get it cleaned up.

RANDY. You'll miss the morning rush. People need their sugar fix.

ARTHUR. Business isn't so hot anyway. That Starbucks is killing me.

RANDY. Your coffee's better.

ARTHUR. I used to ask a quarter for a cup of coffee. Free refills.

RANDY. You replace him yet, the douchebag works here some days?

ARTHUR. No. I put up a sign.

RANDY. You're closed quite a lot lately.

ARTHUR. I haven't felt so hot.

RANDY. You okay?

ARTHUR. Yeah, just.

RANDY. We miss you when you're not here. You're the high point of the day.

ARTHUR. You guys must have some crummy days. *(Pause.)*

RANDY. Hey. Last week. We took a guy in for beating hell out his wife and she give us his Blackhawk tickets.

ARTHUR. Yeah?

RANDY. Blackhawks, Bruins. Great seats.

ARTHUR. Right, you're a big fan, hockey fan.

RANDY. It's the best. I grew up in the middle of seven brothers so I like all sports and all, but hockey's just so *grrr*, you know? Really gets your blood up. *(Beat.)* So I got these two great seats and no one to go with me.

ARTHUR. James won't go with you?

RANDY. Him? We're sick of each other.

ARTHUR. Right.

RANDY. The guy hates sports. Only thing he likes is that *Star Trek*.

ARTHUR. Oh, right —

RANDY. *Voyager, Deep Space Now*, all that shit. Him and his wife watch that shit every night.

ARTHUR. Yeah.

RANDY. Yeah.

ARTHUR. I couldn't do that.

RANDY. No. *(Silence.)* Max told us your wife just died.

ARTHUR. Mm. Ex-wife. Yeah. Yeah, we split up … some years ago.

RANDY. How'd she die?

ARTHUR. Cancer. Yeah, cancer, yeah.

RANDY. Sorry.

ARTHUR. Yeah, thanks.

RANDY. I'm sorry.

ARTHUR. Thanks.

RANDY. My mother died of cancer.

ARTHUR. Mm.

RANDY. Were you there? Were you with her?

ARTHUR. No, I … my … I got a call. She had moved, to North Carolina. I got a call. After she died. My daughter called.

RANDY. I didn't know you had a daughter. *(Someone bangs on the door.)*

ARTHUR. I'm closed.

LADY. *(Offstage.)* What's that?

ARTHUR. I'm closed.

RANDY. It's Lady. She came by a few minutes ago —

ARTHUR. Lady? Is that you?

LADY. *(Offstage.)* Is what me?

ARTHUR. Hold on. *(Arthur opens the door and Lady enters.)* I'm closed today.

LADY. You were closed yesterday.

ARTHUR. I'm closed today too.

RANDY. Hi, Lady.

LADY. Hello.

RANDY. You're out and about early today.

LADY. What's that?

RANDY. I say you're out and about early today.

ARTHUR. Lady's always out and about early. She's an early riser.

LADY. I got a Big Book meetin'. Down at the Rec Room.

RANDY. You doing the meetings?

LADY. What's that?

RANDY. You're still going to your meetings?

LADY. Oh, sure. Every day.

RANDY. How many days sober?

LADY. What's that?

RANDY. How many days do you have sober?

LADY. Just today.

ARTHUR. Try me tomorrow. I should be open tomorrow.

LADY. You're fuckin' with my routine.

ARTHUR. Try me tomorrow.

LADY. Arthur, you don't look good. What's the matter?

ARTHUR. I haven't had any coffee.

LADY. That's a bullshit answer.

ARTHUR. It's a tough day.

LADY. That may be, but don't lose your authenticity, for God's sake.

ARTHUR. Somebody broke in.

LADY. *(Entirely sincere.)* Aww. Good for you, sweetheart. Congratulations. *(Lady exits. Randy stands. Silence.)*

RANDY. So no, James won't go to the Blackhawks game with me.

ARTHUR. That's too bad. *(Silence. James reenters, distributes coffee, cigs.)*

JAMES. I think it froze, just crossing the street.

RANDY. *(Covering.)* You talking about the coffee or your pecker? *(She laughs, too loud.)*

JAMES. Wow. Jesus. Are you ready to go?

RANDY. Yeah.

JAMES. Arthur. Call us if you have any thoughts. *(Randy takes a card from her pocket, gives it to Arthur.)*

RANDY. There's my cell. Give it a ring. *(Beat.)* Maybe you just want to talk. *(Randy and James exit. Arthur looks after them, thinks. He locks the door, turns off lights. Studies Randy's card, tucks it behind the phone on the wall. He takes a cookie tin from under the counter, opens it, rolls a joint from the contents inside. Arthur lights the joint, sits in his darkened shop. The lights shift.)*

ARTHUR. My parents. John and Marie.

They met in a refugee camp, end of the war.

My dad, John. He was in the Polish army, and he ... um, he spent most of the war in a ... as a POW.

My mom was shell-shocked. She must've seen some ... she had to see some just ... Christ, fifteen years old. White Russian farm girl.

They came here ... '49, straight to Jefferson Park.

'Cause of Uncle Wit and Aunt Irene. My parents didn't have any money, couldn't speak the language, Mom was pregnant with me. Borrowed from their brothers and sisters to make a down payment on the shop. They opened in 1950. Year I was born.

Superior Donuts.

Uncle Wit wanted him to call it Przybyszewski Paczki. Dad said Superior was easier to remember and sounds a little like Przybyszewski. And the sign makers charged by the letter. The old man was tight, like all those people, understandably tight.

I asked him "Pop, why'd you open the store in Uptown? Why not Jeff Park?" He said there were too many Polish bakeries on the Northwest Side, and since Uptown was already on the way down they got a good price.

I don't believe it. I think he liked taking the bus.

Weird.

But I think the bus gave the old man a sense of ... industry.

Remember him?

I still see him, bundled up. Stepping out of the house, bitter morning, still dark outside. Hunkered against the wind. Clomping down the icy sidewalk to catch the bus. *(A bang on the door.)* I'm closed.

FRANCO. *(Offstage.)* You're closed. *(Arthur says nothing.)* I'm here about the job. *(Arthur does not respond.)* Hello?

ARTHUR. I'm closed.

FRANCO. *(Offstage.)* Why?

ARTHUR. Chemical spill. Very dangerous. Hazmat team's on the way. Come back tomorrow. *(Long pause. Another bang on the door.)* I'm closed.

FRANCO. *(Offstage.)* Hazmat team. You called about a chemical spill? *(Arthur pinches out his joint, carelessly waves away smoke. Unlocks, opens the door. Franco, backpack on his shoulder, smiles at Arthur.)* Hey, good-lookin'.

ARTHUR. I'm closed.

FRANCO. I'm here about the job. *(Beat.)* You got an opening. *(Arthur studies Franco.)* What do you do?

ARTHUR. I run a donut shop.

FRANCO. I can do that. *(Enters.)* Is it hard?

ARTHUR. No harder than anything else.

FRANCO. How hard is anything else? *(Arthur turns on the light to get a better look at Franco, who takes in the damage.)* Someone fucked up your donut shop. *(Beat.)* I've got work experience. School library, at Truman. I shelve books. *(Beat.)* I'm not in school, not right now. I'm taking a break.

ARTHUR. Taking a break. To work in a donut shop.

FRANCO. What do you have to do?

ARTHUR. Work the counter, serve the food. Brew coffee. Make change.

FRANCO. I ain't gotta make no donuts.

ARTHUR. No.

FRANCO. How come?

ARTHUR. I make the donuts.

FRANCO. So you got this basket here says "bismarck" on it. So say I sell the last bismarck. Then someone comes in here and says they want a bismarck.

ARTHUR. You say we're out of bismarcks.

FRANCO. That's all there is to it.

ARTHUR. Pretty much.

FRANCO. So say someone comes in and they're havin' a party.

ARTHUR. People don't have parties here.

FRANCO. No, they're *gonna* have a party, somewhere else. So they want all the donuts and all the coffee so I sell 'em all the donuts and all the coffee and then there's no more donuts or coffee. What happens the next dude comes in, wants a donut?

ARTHUR. You say you're sorry but we're out of donuts.

FRANCO. But the sign says Superior Donuts. Someone comes in and I say we're out of donuts, that don't look good. I mean if I go into Kentucky Fried Chicken …

ARTHUR. I follow you —

FRANCO. … And they're all outta chicken —

ARTHUR. — Right —

FRANCO. — That's false advertising. You got to think of a thing like that when you name the place. The word *donut* is part of the brand, right? I mean if you called this place House of Wax, and they come in here and they find you done run out of donuts, the customer complaint takes on a different tone. And seein' as you're not here.

ARTHUR. No, I'm here.

FRANCO. No, I mean in the hypothetical.

ARTHUR. Oh, I thought you meant … I thought you meant I wasn't here.

FRANCO. No, I can see you're here.

ARTHUR. Good.

FRANCO. I mean in the hypothetical.

ARTHUR. Right, where someone's —

FRANCO. — Someone's bought all the donuts, you ain't the one gotta bear the brunt of the public reaction.

ARTHUR. What is your *name?*

FRANCO. I'm sayin' if we stick to your system you got to make damn sure we got an abundance of donuts when I'm runnin' the show. Either that, or show me how to make the donuts.

ARTHUR. You *want* to make the donuts.

FRANCO. "Teach a man to fish."

ARTHUR. That's very industrious, but I've had this shop a long time and I've never been caught without donuts and coffee.

FRANCO. You don't allow for the possibility we might get popular and move some donuts up outta here. You're a defeatist.

ARTHUR. What'd you say your name was?

FRANCO. Franco Wicks.

ARTHUR. Franco Wicks. "Franco Wicks."

FRANCO. Who are you?

ARTHUR. I'm Arthur. Przybyszewski.

FRANCO. Arthur S.

ARTHUR. P.

FRANCO. Huh?

ARTHUR. It starts with a P.

FRANCO. It starts with a P.

ARTHUR. Yes.

FRANCO. Say it again.

ARTHUR. *[p]Shub-er-shef-ski.*

FRANCO. I don't hear no P.

ARTHUR. It's in there.

FRANCO. Arthur P. You ain't scammin' me about makin' the donuts, are you? You ain't just shippin' 'em in from Acme Donut Factory.

ARTHUR. I make the donuts. By hand.

FRANCO. You gotta get up early.

ARTHUR. I make the dough in the evening, after I close.

FRANCO. Stick it in the fridge, then fry it up in the morning?

ARTHUR. More flavor that way.

FRANCO. Just flour and oil, right? Then hit it with the sugar?

ARTHUR. No, it's a little more sophisticated than that.

FRANCO. Really sophisticated?

ARTHUR. No, not really.

FRANCO. What kind of oil you use?

ARTHUR. Peanut oil.

FRANCO. Not exactly a healthy choice, is it?

ARTHUR. Could be worse.

FRANCO. Yeah, *could* be. Could be horse fat, but that's not much of an endorsement, is it? You ain't gonna put that on the sign.

ARTHUR. No …

FRANCO. "Superior Donuts … It Ain't Horse Fat!"

ARTHUR. Consider the donut. It's a dessert cake.

FRANCO. A dessert cake?

ARTHUR. Yes.

FRANCO. Or a meal substitute.

ARTHUR. I suppose either one.

FRANCO. Or an *additional* meal. Which contributes to obesity and cardiac disease in the African-American community.

ARTHUR. You're not giving much credit to the discernment of the consumer, African-American or otherwise.

FRANCO. Discernment implies a choice. You don't see no Whole Foods in this neighborhood, do you?

ARTHUR. Oh it's coming. We got a Starbucks right across the street.

FRANCO. Brother, they got Starbucks in wheat fields now. Anyway, you don't see a lot of brothers in the Starbucks, do you? And you ain't never seen a brother in the Whole Foods, unless he's stockin' the shelves. Can you picture that, some big angry black man shoppin' in Whole Foods, his arms all loaded with soy cheese and echinacea and starfruit?

ARTHUR. I wouldn't know.

FRANCO. Why not?

ARTHUR. I don't shop at Whole Foods.

FRANCO. Oh. I do. Shit, I'm just about hooked on that soy cheese.

ARTHUR. Your point is, because no alternative is readily available, I'm contributing to the poor health habits of low-income African-Americans by providing unhealthy meal substitutes?

FRANCO. Well spoke, Arthur P.

ARTHUR. Are you encouraging me to close my business, Franco Wicks?

FRANCO. I'm encouraging you to provide some heart-healthy alternatives. Some fruit or even low-fat bran muffins.

ARTHUR. Bran muffins.

FRANCO. If you want to stay in the world of the donut.

ARTHUR. Hold on, this is your job interview.

FRANCO. How'm I doing?

ARTHUR. No, yeah, pretty good.

FRANCO. Today's your lucky day, Arthur P. I'm a self-starter.

(Arthur studies Franco, considers.)

ARTHUR. Okay, give me a few days to mull it over.

FRANCO. I can start tomorrow.

ARTHUR. Give me a few days.

FRANCO. I can start now.

ARTHUR. You need a job that bad?

FRANCO. I wouldn't waste your time if I didn't.

ARTHUR. You're not in any trouble, are you?

FRANCO. I'm in debt.

ARTHUR. We're only talking about a little help at the counter. Five days a week.

FRANCO. What's the pay?

ARTHUR. Minimum wage.

FRANCO. Which is …

ARTHUR. Eight dollars an hour. It just went up.

FRANCO. How many hours a week?

ARTHUR. Thirty?

FRANCO. Thirty hours a week at eight bucks an hour. Two hundred forty a week. Nine-sixty a month. Little over eleven-five a year. Before taxes.

ARTHUR. Sounds right.

FRANCO. Sounds right? Eleven grand a year sounds right?

ARTHUR. Sounds accurate.

FRANCO. Benefits?

ARTHUR. Such as?

FRANCO. Health insurance?

ARTHUR. Very funny.

FRANCO. Workmen's comp?

ARTHUR. Sure.

FRANCO. Social Security.

ARTHUR. Yeah.

FRANCO. What about profit-sharing?

ARTHUR. Profit-sharing.

FRANCO. Do you believe in profit-sharing?

ARTHUR. Sure, I believe in it. I don't provide it.

FRANCO. What if I can demonstrate an increase in sales?

ARTHUR. We'll talk about that at your first employee evaluation.

FRANCO. Does this mean I got the job? *(Arthur considers another moment ...)*

ARTHUR. Yeah, okay. *(They shake.)*

FRANCO. You won't regret it.

ARTHUR. You live in the neighborhood?

FRANCO. Born and raised, brother. Wilson and Sheridan.

ARTHUR. Live alone?

FRANCO. Nah, I got ... I'm the man in my family. You? From Uptown?

ARTHUR. Jefferson Park. But the shop's been in my family almost sixty years.

FRANCO. I walk past every day of my natural life.

ARTHUR. How come I've never seen you in here?

FRANCO. I don't eat no nasty-ass donuts. But if I'm gonna be workin' here, I better know what the hell I'm sellin', so ... donut, please, and a large coffee.

ARTHUR. Actually, I'm all out of coffee and donuts right now.

(Franco stares at him. During the following, Franco puts on an apron, cleans up the damaged shop. When Franco opens the shades, we see that the shattered glass of the front door has been boarded up. The lights shift.)

A kid. In Chicago. In the '60s. Pure magic. Well. Magic for a white kid, anyway. Christmas windows at Marshall Field's, twilight at Riverview. Another world.

The city was true working class, and the bars were clean and well-lit, and immigrant factory workers would sit and have a beer after a day's work. And sleeping outside with my family, with all the families, on the lawn at Jefferson Park on sticky summer nights. Every Sunday hanging out in someone else's basement, food all day. Or a trip to a forest preserve, all free back then, Polish the only language I'd hear, twenty pigs spinning in fire, and every friend I made became my parents' friend, just because they were my friend. Coming back from a family trip, driving along the Eisenhower, I'd see the giant neon lips of Magikist and I knew I was home.

It changed though. '66. Dr. King was pelted with firecrackers and rocks in Marquette Park. My mom got the old man drunk in the middle of the day to keep him from going down there and shaming us. Maybe that's where the trouble started with the old man.

Then in '68 I got my head cracked open by Daley's police in Old Town, the riot no one saw on TV, the one even more brutal than the others. The old man drove down and bailed me out of County the next morning and didn't say a word to me, which was worse than if he'd socked me one. He just drove me to a recruiting station, parked the car, got out, and walked away. I didn't know what I was supposed to do. I sat and I waited. I waited for my old man to come back to the car. I waited for hours with dried blood in my hair.

It didn't matter.

My notice came in a few weeks anyway and by October I was living in Toronto. *(Lights shift. Arthur and Franco. End of a business day. The graffiti has been covered by a thin coat of paint, but the word "PUSSY" is still visible.)*

FRANCO. You don't talk much, do you? *(Beat.)* Arthur?

ARTHUR. Hm.

FRANCO. You don't talk much. *(Beat.)* Why is that?

ARTHUR. I guess I don't have a lot to say. *(As Franco steps into the kitchen, Kevin Magee enters the shop, approaches the counter. Arthur steps up to serve him.)*

KEVIN. Can I just get a Coke?

ARTHUR. One dollar. *(Arthur gets a can of Coke from the fridge. Kevin pays.)*

KEVIN. Do you have a bag? *(Arthur, vaguely irritated, turns to get a bag from an empty shelf behind him.)*

ARTHUR. Franco? Will you bring me some small paper bags? *(Franco enters from the kitchen with bags. Arthur bags the Coke, gives it to Kevin. Franco cleans counter tops, takes no note of Kevin. But Kevin takes note of Franco, quickly exits.)*

FRANCO. See, you just cost yourself some money. *(Beat.)* 'Cause you don't talk. "Have a nice day." "Thanks for stopping by." "You look like a guy needs more fritter in his diet." That kind of thing. You don't engage the customers.

ARTHUR. He wanted a pop.

FRANCO. He just thinks he wanted a pop. He don't know he wants a fritter. You gotta help him find out.

ARTHUR. Yeah, okay, thanks. *(Arthur clicks off the neon sign, fires up a joint.)*

FRANCO. How come you close so early? *(No response.)* You're missing out on the evening trade. *(Beat.)* Did you know you're missing out on the evening trade?

ARTHUR. I catch some commuters.

FRANCO. They're going home to dinner. They ain't stopping for donuts on their way to dinner. *(Arthur does not respond.)* Do *you* eat donuts for dinner? *(No response.)* Just on weekends maybe, stay open a little later. You might get a coffeehouse atmosphere in here. Like some students tapping away on their laptops or whatever. Get some posters up here for yoga classes and chakra readings. "Release your kundalini energy." Get some art on the walls, make the place a little homier. A family restaurant. For families. And how 'bout some music, brother, can we plug in a radio or some shit?

ARTHUR. A radio, huh?

FRANCO. You can pick the station. All your hits and dusties. I bet we can even find something we both like. Old school.

ARTHUR. Radios interfere with my *quiet time. (Franco seems to take the hint, returns to work ... but the silence becomes oppressive ... and Franco begins to sing, something along the lines of Stevie Wonder. * He begins quietly, but the joy of the song and the point he is making to Arthur move him to sing louder. Arthur watches all of this with dead-*

---

* See Special Note on Songs and Recordings on copyright page.

ARTHUR. No, I want to read it.

FRANCO. No, you don't.

ARTHUR. Please let me read it.

FRANCO. Hell, no.

ARTHUR. Why not?

FRANCO. You wouldn't understand it.

ARTHUR. Is it in English?

FRANCO. You wouldn't get a lot out of my book, Arthur P. I just mean, you know … you run a donut shop.

ARTHUR. Okay.

FRANCO. Don't take it that way. I *work* in a donut shop, so that's why you don't hear me goin' on about writing the Great American Novel.

ARTHUR. You mean you haven't been going on about writing the Great American Novel?

FRANCO. Don't get me started.

ARTHUR. You mean you haven't started?

FRANCO. I can talk about this book *all* goddamn day.

ARTHUR. C'mon, hand it over. I won't criticize.

FRANCO. I don't care about that.

ARTHUR. Then hand it over.

FRANCO. Why you hasslin' me about my book?

ARTHUR. You brought it up!

FRANCO. And then you started hasslin' me about it.

ARTHUR. I'm asking to read it.

FRANCO. 'Cause it's "Be Nice to a Negro Week"?

ARTHUR. You said I *didn't* want to read it 'cause you're black.

FRANCO. And now the *only* reason you want to read it is 'cause I'm black.

ARTHUR. I don't care that you're black!

FRANCO. Well you should. *Proud* black man.

ARTHUR. Franco. Regardless of your skin color, yet in acknowledgment of your estimable heritage, I'm asking to read your book.

FRANCO. 'Cause you're so crazy about "Afro-American" literature? What, you read *The Autobiography of Malcolm X* and so now you know all about the Experience? They made you read Langston Hughes in school and now you're an expert? Can you name any black poets other than Langston Hughes?

ARTHUR. Yeah, in fact, I can.

FRANCO. Go.

ARTHUR. Is this a test?

FRANCO. Yeah. This is a test. This is your racist test.

ARTHUR. I have to take a racist test.

FRANCO. You said you weren't no racist.

ARTHUR. Do you have to take a racist test?

FRANCO. You better reread Malcolm, Arthur P. I can't be a racist. I'm the oppressed. *(A moment. An appraisal. Then ...)* Five bucks says you can't pass my test.

ARTHUR. Make it a sawbuck.

FRANCO. Get your money on the table, sucker. *(They produce tens, put them on the table.)* Okay. Okay, the test is ... name ten black poets.

ARTHUR. Ten.

FRANCO. Yep.

ARTHUR. That's not a racist test, it's a *poet* test.

FRANCO. I'll even throw in Langston, all right, he can be Number One. Go. Ten poets. If you say Nipsey Russell, the game is over.

ARTHUR. Langston Hughes.

FRANCO. That's a gimme. One.

ARTHUR. Maya Angelou.

FRANCO. Yeah, you saw her on *Oprah*. Good for you, that's two.

ARTHUR. Gwendolyn Brooks.

FRANCO. Sure, Chicago blood. Three.

ARTHUR. Countee Cullen.

FRANCO. Oh, now that's a good one. I'm impressed. You just answered the four black poets who might be in your crossword puzzle. But it gets tougher now. *(Arthur stares into space, thinking. Franco cracks up.)* Brother, you are finished.

ARTHUR. Don't goad me. Give me a second. *(Arthur stands, thinking.)*

FRANCO. Don't hurt yourself now.

ARTHUR. Give me a second. *(Arthur thinks.)*

FRANCO. Dang, Arthur, your head's about to split open.

ARTHUR. C'mon ...

FRANCO. Your brain's gonna fall out on the floor.

ARTHUR. Oh, wait, what is his name?

FRANCO. Here comes Nipsey.

ARTHUR. Shh. *(A long silence.)*

FRANCO. It's like watching George Bush on *Jeopardy*.

ARTHUR. The names will come to me.

FRANCO. *(Holding up the two tens.)* You don't want to bump up the bet, do you? By a couple of million dollars?

ARTHUR. If I pass the test, you let me read your book.

FRANCO. If you can't, you let me try out my coffeehouse idea.

ARTHUR. Deal. Where were we?

FRANCO. Just four —

ARTHUR. *(Rapid fire.)* Alice Walker, Ntozake Shange, Amiri Baraka, Lucille Clifton, Nikki Giovanni, and Yusef Komunyakaa. *(Arthur snaps the money from Franco's hand, heads behind the counter. Franco stands, frozen. Arthur turns to Franco … and smiles, winks. Max enters.)*

MAX. Arthur.

ARTHUR. Hey, Max.

MAX. Coffee, please. This is your new man?

ARTHUR. Franco. Franco Wicks.

MAX. Franco. Like the Generalissimo?

FRANCO. No, like Franco Harris.

MAX. Franco Harris?

FRANCO. Pittsburgh Steelers? C'mon, man, Franco Harris? The Immaculate Reception?

MAX. The immaculate *reception?* There was an immaculate *reception?* We have different Bible, I guess, you and me. Mine only has immaculate *conception.*

FRANCO. They ain't the same thing.

MAX. No. I would not think so.

FRANCO. No, see, 'cause the Immaculate Reception is something that actually *happened.*

MAX. So. Arthur. You employ demon worshippers to sell your donuts. Speaking of, give me a dozen donuts, please, for the boys from Nizhny.

ARTHUR. The work's going okay?

MAX. They are good boys, good at their work, but I think their new country distract them. They are not used to so many black people, no offense. And the girls, too, they cannot keep their eyes from pretty girls.

ARTHUR. They must see pretty girls in Russia, too.

FRANCO. Yeah, but no "bleck people."

MAX. *(Ignoring Franco.)* Oh yes, very pretty. But American girls, they do that thing, they have that sassy thing they do, they have confident way, they have equal way that women in Russia will never have. This boy, my oldest sister's oldest boy, Kiril he is called, he fall in love with lady bartender. She is very tough and she wears boots and a black watch on wrist and she calls Kiril "baby" and "honey." And now he is there every night, drinking one beer for four hours, and staring with big eyes at this bartender. So he comes in to work in mornings and he has no strength, he cannot lift particle board. I say, "Kiril, have you told this bartender you love her?" He says, "No, because she will laugh at me and then I cannot go back and look at her no more." I say, "Would that be a bad thing? Would you want to look at this woman if she laugh at you?" He says, "If I cannot look at her, I will pray for God to kill me." *(Max laughs. Arthur and Franco do not.)* It's more funny how you say it in Russian. So no, work is slow because boys cannot stop thinking about it. As they must. And by the way, Arthur, I can still see your "pussy." *(Max refers to the spray-painted wall.)*

ARTHUR. You can still read it, can't you?

MAX. It looks like today's special.

ARTHUR. Franco, can you put another coat on that? *(Franco exits to the back room.)*

MAX. Arthur, sell me this store. I am desperate!

ARTHUR. Sorry, Max.

MAX. I give you good price! I give you same price I offer before Wall Street douchebags fuck everyone in the ass.

ARTHUR. It's not for sale.

MAX. But is so important for me. I expanse my business for electronics next, plasma, HD, Blu-ray, all digital everything. Nola says she will sell me nail salon, but it does me no good if you take up space in between. With that footage? Mine *and* you *and* Nola? A corner lot? I would be biggest electronics shop in Uptown.

ARTHUR. Until they open a Best Buy on the other side of Broadway.

MAX. Let them try. Best Buy cannot do business against me. I offer something Best Buy will never have.

ARTHUR. Which is?

MAX. The personal touch. And Croatian pornography.

ARTHUR. Maybe Uptown would miss my personal touch.

MAX. Arthur, no one come! You sell donut and no one wants donut anymore! People now, they eat yogurt and banana, not donut. And people who want donut can go to Duckin' Donut and eat the shit cake! If they want coffee, they go to Starbuck and pay four dollars for caramel fuck-a-cheeto. You are only donut shop on North Side, you have said this. All the others close. Why? Because they are selling product no one want! Donut is like videotape, it is over! Time change everything, and donut has been left behind.

ARTHUR. Time hasn't changed me. *(Franco reenters from the back room, carrying paint and brush. During the following, he opens the can, mixes paint, starts to apply a second coat to the spray-painted wall.)*

MAX. Maybe not. But people still *can*, can always change later. Donut cannot change. Donut will always be donut.

FRANCO. "Donut will always be donut."

MAX. Come on, how much you think shop should sell? I mean real estate only. One hundred sixty thousand? One sixty-five?

ARTHUR. It doesn't really matter —

MAX. *(A real explosion.)* Goddamn it, I need this store! *(Arthur and Franco are taken aback.)* I have plans for my life. I have a picture in my head of what my life should be, and that picture look more and more like fairy tale. I am almost fifty years old. My hair has disappear and my breasts are falling to Earth and *still,* I rent my home from old Jewish woman. I cannot ask any woman to be my wife in a rented home. Almost *fifty.* These boys from Nizhny, they think I am homosexual because I am still bachelor. I'm embarrassed. I come to this country to make a mark, not fade away.

ARTHUR. I'm sorry, but my store is not for sale.

MAX. Believe me: Day will come you wish you take my good price.

ARTHUR. *(With irony.)* Donuts are my life.

MAX. Donuts are not your life. Donuts are not anybody's life. Your life is your life. A home. A home of your own, that is life. A home and children and a wife. *(The room goes icy.)* I'm sorry, Arthur.

ARTHUR. Don't worry about it. Here's your donuts.

MAX. No, I feel very foolish. I was not thinking about your wife.

ARTHUR. Max. Please stop.

MAX. What has got inside me? These boys! Seeing these boys see this country for first time has got my insides all worked up. I remember first time for me, in America ... my eyes blur just to think about it. Just to remember so much ... *(Re: donuts and coffee.)* How much for these?

ARTHUR. On the house.

MAX. No, Arthur —

ARTHUR. Tell the boys from Nizhny to enjoy.

MAX. I will tell them it is American hospitality.

ARTHUR. Tell them it's Polish hospitality.

MAX. *That* they will never believe. *(Max exits.)*

FRANCO. How you know them poets, man?

ARTHUR. I —

FRANCO. You're a damn hustler!

ARTHUR. I'm a reader, that's all.

FRANCO. Are you like one of those idiot-savants?

ARTHUR. Yeah, probably.

FRANCO. You're cold-blooded is what you are. *(Franco hands his book to Arthur.)* You got to take real good care of this. 'Cause I don't have any other copies. I just now finished it so I haven't had it typed or put on a computer. *(Beat.)* No one's read it yet.

ARTHUR. I'm the first.

FRANCO. You're the first. *(A moment between them. Franco resumes his paint job as Arthur tends to the register. Franco laughs.)* Way you just rattled them off? Cold-blooded. Like you was Rain Man, only entertaining. Hey, tell me you ain't sellin' this place to that Russian cracker.

ARTHUR. What's it to you? *(Franco shrugs.)*

FRANCO. What's that about your wife? Are you married?

ARTHUR. No.

FRANCO. I thought Max just said —

ARTHUR. Max talks a lot. *(Silence.)*

FRANCO. Divorced.

ARTHUR. Yes.

FRANCO. Recent?

ARTHUR. Let's just. Skip it. Okay?

FRANCO. Okay. *(Beat.)* So you're single these days.

ARTHUR. Yeah.

FRANCO. Yeah, me too. Kinda. Yeah. How come you don't go out with that lady cop?

ARTHUR. Why would I do that?

FRANCO. She's sure into you. I seen her when she comes by, I think she wants to drink a big tub of your bath water. And I wish I hadn't said that cause I just got a little sick in my mouth.

ARTHUR. You're crazy.

FRANCO. You hadn't noticed.

ARTHUR. She's just friendly.

FRANCO. No, *I'm* friendly. She's good to go.

ARTHUR. It. I. I.

FRANCO. Pick a verb, any verb.

31

ARTHUR. I haven't dated in a long time.

FRANCO. That's hard to believe, way you dress and everything.

ARTHUR. What do you mean?

FRANCO. Nothing.

ARTHUR. What's wrong with the way I dress?

FRANCO. C'mon now. Look at yourself. I hate to break it to you, but the Grateful Dead ain't gonna hire a new guitar player. That old man died and they just called it quits.

ARTHUR. I like to be comfortable.

FRANCO. You might be comfortable *naked,* but that don't mean it looks good.

ARTHUR. You're not really a fashion plate yourself.

FRANCO. I ain't goin' out with no lady cop.

ARTHUR. Neither am I.

FRANCO. Suit yourself.

ARTHUR. What would you suggest?

FRANCO. First of all, the ponytail has got to go.

ARTHUR. Now stop right there.

FRANCO. Let me tell you who looks good in a ponytail: girls … *and ponies.*

ARTHUR. I've had this ponytail almost forty years, man.

FRANCO. And you ain't ashamed yet?

ARTHUR. You've got a mean streak, you know it?

FRANCO. I'd lose the T-shirts. Get you some shirts button down the front, hide your belly a bit. And it might be time for some new jeans. Y'know what, let me rephrase that: Might be time to soak those in jet fuel, light a match and run for your goddamn life.

ARTHUR. These are my lucky jeans. *(Franco stares at him.)*

FRANCO. Get you some good shoes. And not tennis shoes, neither, unless you're gonna play tennis. And shave that nasty-ass beard. And wash your hair. And get a new coat. And get some glasses don't have tape and shit on them. And trim your eyebrows. And stop carrying shit around in plastic shopping bags, you look like a homeless man. Get a leather bag or light backpack. And cut your fingernails. Lose that earring. And throw out all those white tube socks. And here's a tip about patchouli: It smells like cat piss.

ARTHUR. I don't use patchouli.

FRANCO. Then it's time to get rid of that cat.

ARTHUR. Is that it? *(Franco studies Arthur, thinks.)*

FRANCO. Did I say trim your eyebrows?

ARTHUR. Yes.

FRANCO. Then yeah, that's it.

ARTHUR. Didn't know you had such a strong reaction to my appearance.

FRANCO. Ain't nothing to me. You do what you want. But if you want that lady cop to frisk you, you better clean up your act.

ARTHUR. You really think she digs me, huh?

FRANCO. Why do you think she keeps "following up" on the Scarlet Pussy here? I've been here four days and she's already stuck her nose in here *twice*, "Oh hey, just wonder if you had any thoughts about who might've done this, just wonder if you heard anything, just following up." You'd think Lindbergh's baby got swiped out of your donut shop. She needs you to make the first move, though. She's at least got that much self-respect.

ARTHUR. I don't know how to do that.

FRANCO. Are you telling me you really don't know what to say to that sad, middle-age, milky-gray lady cop?

ARTHUR. She's a *cop*; a day in her life is more interesting than a year in a donut shop.

FRANCO. Then you tell her about your colonoscopy.

ARTHUR. I haven't had a colonoscopy.

FRANCO. Well, you really should have a colonoscopy. We can talk about that later. Tell her how you feel about disco. Tell her why you think it's wrong for the Catholic Church to sanction pedophilia.

ARTHUR. Oh Jesus —

FRANCO. Tell her who you voted for president. Like there's any doubt.

ARTHUR. Like I voted.

FRANCO. Say what?

ARTHUR. The fix is in, Franco. I found that out forty years ago.

FRANCO. Okay, so don't tell her that 'cause you're just so sad and bleak and hopeless you make us all want to go kill ourselves. *Talk about donuts.*

ARTHUR. Donuts.

FRANCO. I guess if you know so damn much about black poets, you might know a thing or two about donuts. *The History of the Donut* by Arthur Shubber-somethin'. Look at you. All worked up over some female lady. *(Arthur frets.)* Hey. Arthur P. *(Arthur looks at Franco. Quiet encouragement.)* It's cool, man. Go for it. *(Beat.)* She's good-lookin', don't you think?

ARTHUR. You just said she's "milky-gray."

FRANCO. I just mean she's good-lookin' for *you*. She's single, she ain't no fatty, she's got a good job — well, maybe not a *good* job, but she ain't moppin' up a donut shop. Seems like there aren't too many entanglements.

ARTHUR. There's always entanglements.

FRANCO. She doesn't have any kids, does she?

ARTHUR. I don't think so.

FRANCO. *You* don't have any kids, do you?

ARTHUR. Mm.

FRANCO. *Do* you?

ARTHUR. I have a daughter.

FRANCO. No shit. How old?

ARTHUR. She just turned nineteen.

FRANCO. Nineteen. You got a picture?

ARTHUR. I don't think so. I gotta get to the bank. How's that cleanup coming?

FRANCO. Come on, man, you don't carry a picture of your own daughter?

ARTHUR. I really. I don't want to talk about this.

FRANCO. Why?

ARTHUR. Franco. Would you mind.

FRANCO. Mind what.

ARTHUR. Just. I'd just like to keep things here on the … I don't want to talk about this stuff —

FRANCO. Keep things here on the what? *(Beat.)* You want to keep things here on the what?

ARTHUR. *(Taking check from till.)* What is this? Did you take a personal check?

FRANCO. Yeah.

ARTHUR. I don't take personal checks. I told you I don't take personal checks. Some hard-luck story bought twenty dollars worth of donuts?

FRANCO. No.

ARTHUR. You didn't give cash back.

FRANCO. She said she needed food for her three babies!

ARTHUR. Did she buy anything?

FRANCO. A Long John.

ARTHUR. You gave her nineteen dollars back?

FRANCO. She's good for it. The check'll clear.

ARTHUR. If it doesn't? You'll make up the difference?

FRANCO. Yeah, right. I'll make up the difference when you start paying into my 401(k).

ARTHUR. Don't take any more checks.

FRANCO. You give a free donut to that old winehead comes in here, every day.

ARTHUR. Lady is different.

FRANCO. How's she different? She ain't got no babies.

ARTHUR. She's different 'cause I say she's different. Because this is my store and I can give away anything I want to. You can't.

FRANCO. I just asked to see a picture of your daughter —

ARTHUR. I'm not talking about this stuff. And I'm not paying you to talk about this stuff, or turn my shop into some nightclub. Or cut off my ponytail. I'm paying you to sell donuts. *(The lights shift and Arthur continues his story.)*

What I did is called "evasion." Not resistance. Draft evaders are different from draft resisters.

And what's the difference?

The fight is the difference. Resisters fight. Evaders evade.

Toronto in '68, '69. The whole bit. The Annex neighborhood, Brunswick Avenue. I wrote a couple of articles for our hairy little newspaper. I sat in a basement with other members of the Union of American Exiles, howling about Mao while we nursed our American hangovers.

We were informed, we were angry, we were righteous. We knew this war was flat fucking wrong.

We were all keeping a big secret, too:

We were scared.

I was ashamed of it then.

Maybe I'm ashamed of it now.

But really …

What could be more human …

To be scared …

To keep it a secret … *(Luther Flynn enters, followed by Kevin.)*

LUTHER. Franco.

ARTHUR. Sorry, I'm closed.

LUTHER. I'm sorry, I'm really here just to see Franco.

FRANCO. *(To Arthur.)* It's cool, he's a friend of mine. *(Arthur exits to the kitchen, grabs his coat.)*

LUTHER. Mary Mother of God, where's the heater in this joint?

35

My blood is frozen. *(Arthur reenters, zips up a money bag.)*

ARTHUR. I gotta get to the bank before seven. You good until seven?

FRANCO. Moppin' it up over here, boss. *(The four men consider each other for an awkward moment. Arthur exits. Franco and Luther hug.)*

LUTHER. Great to see you.

FRANCO. You too.

LUTHER. You remember Kevin? He was out there at Hawthorne with us some.

KEVIN. *(Presses a handshake.)* How's it goin'?

FRANCO. Yeah, good.

LUTHER. Where you been?

FRANCO. I been around.

LUTHER. I haven't seen you. I thought for sure we'd see you over at the club for the Breeder's Cup. Grady had a big thing, with barbecue, all the nuts. It was okay.

FRANCO. I been too tapped out.

LUTHER. Tell me about it. I got my ass handed to me last couple months.

FRANCO. Yeah?

KEVIN. Big Ten's been a bloodbath.

LUTHER. Every fucking thing, the Series set me back a good chunk and I been playing catch up ever since. Then all of a sudden Notre Dame decides to play ball and I gotta pay off every mackerelsnapper this side of South Bend. Fucking freak show.

FRANCO. Times are tough.

LUTHER. Times are tough. Times are tough. How 'bout you? You doing okay?

FRANCO. No, I. Hey, I'm working here, so you see how I am.

KEVIN. Yeah, you're working in this donut shop.

FRANCO. Yeah, for now.

LUTHER. We're the last of the working men.

KEVIN. What do you get here, like minimum?

LUTHER. Last time I saw you though, you had something else working, right? Some crazy thing about, what was it, *gold?*

FRANCO. Yeah, no, that fell through —

KEVIN. What, like a — you had a treasure map?

LUTHER. *(Laughs.)* Right, it was like a treasure map, and the X marked the spot.

KEVIN. Where you found the buried treasure —

LUTHER. Gold doubloons.

FRANCO. No, it wasn't … it doesn't matter —

LUTHER. I'm just bustin' your hump. Christ, at least you're trying. That's why I love you, kid, you're always working some Chinese angle. What do you got for me?

FRANCO. Not much.

KEVIN. What is not much?

LUTHER. How much?

FRANCO. Three hundred.

LUTHER. Jeez, Franco, that's rough on me, y'know? I mean I got Grady snapping at my heels. The wolves are at the door.

FRANCO. I'm sorry, Luther, that's what I got.

LUTHER. I hate this. Y'know? I mean I really hate it. You and me? But I'm in a tough spot.

FRANCO. I hear you.

LUTHER. You don't act like it. And then you disappear on me.

FRANCO. I didn't disappear.

LUTHER. When's the last time you're in the club?

FRANCO. I had to come up with a new plan.

KEVIN. The Donut Plan.

FRANCO. That's why I got this shitty gig, just 'cause I figured something is better than nothing.

LUTHER. You're into me for sixteen K, Frank. Three yards just won't cut it.

FRANCO. Okay …

LUTHER. So you tell me, what else can we do about this?

FRANCO. Extend my credit. Give me the Bears on Sunday. Double or nothing.

LUTHER. That's how we got into this mess. I knew better than to let you double down at eight but I was doin' you a solid. It's over now; I can't do it. Cutler tanks and you're into me for thirty-two thousand and that can't happen. Anyway, you want to gamble on paper only and I need cash in hand, right?

KEVIN. Meanwhile the juice is adding up.

LUTHER. That's right, our debts just get bigger, yours and mine.

FRANCO. I'd lay it off with another bookie if I could —

KEVIN. If you could find someone who'll let you bet sixteen grand that you don't have. And you can't find that.

LUTHER. Credit's dried up all over.

KEVIN. And word's out on you.

LUTHER. And word's out on you, Frank. So what are we going to do about this situation? 'Cause I'm worried.

FRANCO. Let it ride, double or nothing, one more week.

KEVIN. The fuck.

FRANCO. Let it ride. Bears plus three-and-a-half. *(Luther winces, grabs his stomach.)*

LUTHER. Got any milk? *(Franco gets Luther a glass of milk.)* Ulcer. Like I swallowed a hot coal. My wife's sister showed up at the apartment last week, from Puerto Rico, left her husband or he kicked her out, some fucking thing, nobody has a job, brought her two kids with her. They're living in our dining room, for Christ's sake, got their toys spread out all over. I wake up in the morning and all I hear all day is these electronic video games and computers. I live with robots. I said, "Marisol, for the love of God, your sister can't afford to rent a place for her and her kids but she's got more electronics than NASA." My wife bawled me out. *You* know Marisol: "Chu got no caring is what. Chu got no *empathy*." I said, "Why do you think I got an ulcer? What do you think gave it to me?" She says smoking cigars and eating Italian beef. I say, "No, it's empathy."

KEVIN. Right.

LUTHER. I got a hole in my stomach because I take on the worries of the world. That's my problem, Franco: It's empathy. Your worries are my worries. You can't come up with a solution to your problem and it makes the hole in my stomach get that much bigger. So let's get practical here. How about your mom? Can you hit her up for it?

FRANCO. Luther, my mom is livin' on a government check. I pay for her and my baby sister.

LUTHER. C'mon, nothing stashed in the coffee can for a rainy day?

FRANCO. No way. I'm doing everything I can to get us out of that dump we're in.

LUTHER. And you don't know where your old man is.

KEVIN. There's a shocker.

FRANCO. *(Ignoring Kevin.)* No, I don't hear from him.

LUTHER. Grannies? Uncles? Aunties?

FRANCO. No.

LUTHER. How about the teachers over at your old school, at Truman, none of them are — ?

FRANCO. No, we don't keep in touch.

LUTHER. Neighborhood buddies.

FRANCO. Nope … *(Luther stares at Franco.)*

LUTHER. You're very negative, Frank. *(Beat.)* Okay. Here's the deal. I don't have the inclination to jump on you and start whackin' you on the head. *(Points to Kevin.)* But he does. Grady is coming down on me hard and before I take a beating from him, you'll take a beating from Kev. And I don't mean love taps. We're gonna get serious, and you know what that means. I don't like it, but … that's your incentive. I don't care if you got to walk into Bank of America with your momma's pantyhose on your head and your pickle in your hand. I need my fucking money. I need to get paid. *(Silence.)* I'm embarrassed.

KEVIN. Don't be. *(Arthur enters.)*

LUTHER. Let's go. *(To Franco.)* See you about a week. *(Arthur exits to the kitchen. Kevin whacks Franco collegially on the shoulder …)*

KEVIN. I can't wait to see you again. (… *And exits. Luther shrugs apologetically.)*

LUTHER. Nothing personal, kid. *(Luther exits. Arthur reenters.)*

ARTHUR. What's all that about?

FRANCO. Just some friends …

ARTHUR. That didn't seem too friendly.

FRANCO. Yeah, well. You're not paying me to talk about this stuff. You're paying me to sell donuts.

ARTHUR. Right … *(Franco shoulders his backpack, exits. Lights shift.)*

Dad dropped dead. Right here, right where I'm standing. May Day, 1970. Three days before the National Guard murdered four kids at Kent State University. Wonder what the old man would have said about that.

What did you do?

Couldn't come to the funeral. Mom sent photos. Including a snap of two guys from the FBI. Just looking around. Looking around at my father's funeral. That seems weird, they'd send someone just for me. But they did.

What did you do, where did you go?

Further away. Split Toronto, headed up to the Great Slave Lake, outside Yellowknife, in the Northwest Territory.

What did you do?

Cut timber and read a lot of books. Until President Carter

invited me home.

What did you do?

Caught a cab at Midway, had the driver take me directly to the cemetery. Stared at the old man's headstone there in St. Adalbert's. Remembered the last word he ever said to me: coward.

Coward.

End of Act One

ACT TWO

A bitter Chicago dawn.

Sounds: approaching rumble of a bus ... brake whine ... bus door opening ... bus recedes.

Arthur enters the shop carrying his plastic grocery bags. He opens the radiator valve, prepares for the workday.

Moments later, Franco enters, frozen. He goes about the routine of opening the shop.

Tension. Arthur wants to initiate conversation, but Franco is all business.

Activity without speaking for at least one full minute ... perhaps two.

Arthur removes Franco's book from his grocery bags, sets it on the counter between them.

ARTHUR. I read it.
FRANCO. That was fast.
ARTHUR. It's a quick read.
FRANCO. And?
ARTHUR. It's really impressive, Franco.
FRANCO. You think?
ARTHUR. Yeah.
FRANCO. Really?
ARTHUR. It's really something.
FRANCO. No. Really?
ARTHUR. No. Really. I'm impressed.
FRANCO. Really?
ARTHUR. I just think it's great.

FRANCO. Arthur P. You. You just. You.

ARTHUR. Pick a verb, any verb.

FRANCO. You just … sit right down and tell me every little thing you can think to say about it.

ARTHUR. It's completely engaging, from start to finish.

FRANCO. Engaging, you mean in the sense you were *interested.*

ARTHUR. Yeah.

FRANCO. You were *engaged*, it was *engaging, yes!* Okay, what else?

ARTHUR. From start to finish, I was really swept along by the story.

FRANCO. "Swept along by the story." Arthur P. says: "Swept Along by The Story."

ARTHUR. The writing, really. I would never believe it was written by someone so young. I just can't think of enough good things to say about it. It's just great. *(A long moment.)*

FRANCO. Did you like Rocco, the main character?

ARTHUR. Rocco Biggs is just a great character.

FRANCO. Yeah?

ARTHUR. He's funny and smart, and we cheer for him, y'know? We want to know he's going to be okay. That's what keeps us reading.

FRANCO. Right.

ARTHUR. That chapter about his dad, that's a killer.

FRANCO. Which one, you mean when his —

ARTHUR. Well, that whole section really, at the racetrack, after his dad gets in trouble and you know he has to blow town —

FRANCO. — Right —

ARTHUR. — And he sits Rocco down and you know this is really the last time they'll ever see each other, and he tells Rocco this is really it. He's not going to be around anymore.

FRANCO. Yeah.

ARTHUR. And that if Rocco wants to survive in America, he's got to just keep hustling, keep, what is it he says? The little mantra he gives him?

FRANCO. "Never stop moving."

ARTHUR. That's it.

FRANCO. "Never stop moving."

ARTHUR. I think you should show this to some people.

FRANCO. What do you mean? Who?

ARTHUR. Get it typed up or put on a computer or whatever, then show it to I don't know, a publisher, or an editor.

FRANCO. No shit?

ARTHUR. No, I'm serious. I mean you have to clean it up, right, no one wants to go through all these legal pads and —
FRANCO. Right, right, right, right —
ARTHUR. — But no, get it cleaned up and then find someone who does this sort of thing.
FRANCO. You know anybody?
ARTHUR. What do you mean?
FRANCO. You know anybody who does that sort of thing?
ARTHUR. You mean the *typing?*
FRANCO. No, man, the publishing. You know any publishers?
ARTHUR. No. How would I know publishers? No.
FRANCO. You don't know anyone like that?
ARTHUR. No. Hey, don't let that stop you. You know what, I get the feeling you won't let that stop you. You'll find someone.
FRANCO. Thanks, Arthur.
ARTHUR. I haven't done anything.
FRANCO. Just that you read it. Y'know? Means a lot.
ARTHUR. Thanks for letting me read it.
FRANCO. You won the bet, fair and square. *(Beat.)* Nah. I wanted you to read it.
ARTHUR. I guess it's not real unless someone else reads it.
FRANCO. That ain't it. Just. Well, that's what friends do, right? They share their stories. *(Arthur takes this in ... seems to want to respond. Lights shift.)*
ARTHUR. Magda asked me to talk. She begged me to talk, begged me to fight, but I couldn't do it. I can't say why. And I can't say why because I don't know why.

Magda was the daughter of a family friend. I met her at my mom's wake, 1988, and we hit it off. Maybe that doesn't sound too romantic, but wakes can be heady stuff, especially to us, to the Polish. The root of the Polish character is hopelessness. A wake is proof; death is confirmation. The old ladies take the mourner by the arm and guide him straight to the casket and gesture at the body as if to say, *"See?"*

We came from similar backgrounds. We knew some of the same people. We were neighbors. When I asked her to marry me, it was a comfortable notion. "Hey, I really dig you and you dig me too and so maybe we should get married." Comfortable.

It's easy to underrate that now, but there's nothing wrong with comfort, you know? You're lying in a bed in the city of Chicago and you have your arms wrapped around a person who's made the decision to move through the world with you. That may be comfort and not much more, but it may be love, too … *(Light shift. Arthur, Randy. Uncomfortable silence.)*

RANDY. Wow. You really know your donut history.

ARTHUR. Yeah. And that's just the *American* side of the story. The *French* have a donut they call *pet de nonne*, which means "Nun's Fart." The story is that a young nun living in an abbey was preparing a meal when she suddenly … emitted flatus. The other nuns laughed at her and she was so startled that she dropped a ball of dough into a bubbling cauldron, accidentally inventing the donut.

RANDY. Huh.

ARTHUR. Yeah. The *French*.

RANDY. Emitted flatus.

ARTHUR. Right? *(Franco, with dough-covered hands, enters from the kitchen in a cloud of flour. He hands Arthur one tiny wrinkled donut on a small plate.)*

FRANCO. Eat that. *(Arthur tries the donut.)*

ARTHUR. Little overdone. *(Franco exits to the kitchen.)*

RANDY. Got him cooking, huh?

ARTHUR. He's been messing with the dough for a few days, trying to get that just right. But today's his first day at the fryer.

RANDY. Big day. *(An awkward silence.)*

ARTHUR. Do you want a donut?

RANDY. What's good today?

ARTHUR. Everything's the same. Not the same as everything else. The same as it always is.

RANDY. What's your favorite?

ARTHUR. I don't eat them so often. *(Off her disappointment.)* Cinnamon. Cinnamon's the most fresh. The freshest. The most recent. I made the dough the most recent of the doughs I made so the cinnamon is … the freshest.

RANDY. Okay. I'll have a cinnamon. *(He serves her a donut.)* Franco make this?

ARTHUR. No no. He's a long way from edible.

RANDY. You make the dough from scratch?

ARTHUR. By hand. Every evening.

RANDY. I bet not a lot of people do that anymore.

ARTHUR. It's a dying art.

FRANCO. *(Offstage.)* YEE-OWW, GODDAMN IT, MOTHER-FUCKIN' PEANUT OIL GETS HOT!

ARTHUR. Would you like some coffee?

RANDY. Yeah, sure. *(He pours her a cup of coffee.)*

ARTHUR. How was your game?

RANDY. What?

ARTHUR. The Blackhawks.

RANDY. Oh, right. I didn't go.

ARTHUR. Oh.

RANDY. Yeah, I gave the tickets to my brother Mike.

ARTHUR. That's too bad.

RANDY. Yeah.

ARTHUR. That's too bad.

RANDY. Hey.

ARTHUR. Mm. *(An awkward silence.)* I better check on Franco. *(Arthur exits to the kitchen. We can't hear their conversation, but Franco heatedly kicks Arthur out ... concluding, possibly, with, "Get out there and talk to that girl." Arthur reenters.)* Where's James?

RANDY. On the phone with his wife. They've got a convention coming up. *Star Trek* convention.

ARTHUR. Convention, wow.

RANDY. Yeah, they get all dressed up like characters from the show.

ARTHUR. James dresses up?

RANDY. Yeah, pointy ears, the whole shebang.

ARTHUR. Whatever gets you through the night.

RANDY. He's a total nerd and a freakin' idiot but it's kinda sweet that he and his wife do all that together, y'know? No matter what losers they are, at least they got each other. My whole family is guys, right, all of 'em cops. My dad was a cop, and six of my seven brothers are cops, and so all my life it's been cops and sports and whiskey and all that good Irish horseshit, and I love it and everything, that's my home, y'know, that's who I am. But I don't know, I used to wish I didn't always have to be in the club. I thought wouldn't it be nice if I got to be who I wanted to be and maybe someone could come and join in with me for a change.

ARTHUR. Yeah ...

RANDY. I don't know.

ARTHUR. No, I ... yeah. *(An awkward silence.)*

RANDY. *(Re: donut.)* Really good.

RANDY. Good coffee, too — Hm?

ARTHUR. Y'know I think I —

ARTHUR. No, sorry.

RANDY. No, go ahead.

ARTHUR. No, you.

RANDY. No, I was just, I just said "Good coffee."

ARTHUR. It is good.

RANDY. Yes.

ARTHUR. I mean, "Is it good?"

RANDY. Yes. So you were saying.

ARTHUR. I ... *(A long painful silence.)* I don't remember. *(Franco enters with a plate which holds an ugly ball of dough.)*

FRANCO. Eat that. *(Arthur tries the donut.)*

ARTHUR. Yeah, that's hot raw dough. *(James enters.)*

JAMES. Arthur. Give me a large coffee, please, extra cream, extra sugar. Hey, Franco. How's your mom?

FRANCO. She's good.

JAMES. Tell her I said hi.

ARTHUR. You guys know each other?

JAMES. All black folks know each other. Didn't you know that? *(Arthur looks to Franco, who nods. To Arthur.)* Franco's mom worked with my mom in the cafeteria. High school, at Senn. *(To Franco.)* You're not in college anymore? Weren't you going to Loyola?

FRANCO. Truman.

JAMES. I thought you were at Loyola.

FRANCO. Just for a semester.

JAMES. Then you went to Truman.

FRANCO. Yeah.

JAMES. You drop out?

FRANCO. I had to take a break.

JAMES. Why'd you do that?

FRANCO. Had to get a job.

JAMES. Don't stay out too long. You let too much time go by and you won't go back.

FRANCO. No, I'm going back, I just need to make some scratch.

JAMES. I hear that. *(Franco exits to the kitchen.)*

RANDY. How's Crystal, she got your little costume all picked out for your little convention?

JAMES. Oh, man ...

RANDY. She get your little pointy ears all sharpened?

JAMES. *(To Arthur.)* I had a beer over at Carol's Pub last night. Know who I ran into?

ARTHUR. Ray Klapprott. That's his hang-out.

JAMES. He tells me you two didn't part on such good terms.

ARTHUR. Yeah, I suppose.

JAMES. Suppose he's the one who vandalized your store?

ARTHUR. Nah.

JAMES. You sure? What was your fight about?

ARTHUR. No, we didn't have a fight.

JAMES. He called it a fight.

ARTHUR. It wasn't a *fight*.

JAMES. You don't want to say.

RANDY. No, he doesn't want to say.

ARTHUR. No, it's not like that, we just … it was political.

JAMES. He made it sound personal.

ARTHUR. Same thing, man.

JAMES. No, reason it got me thinking about the writing on your wall there … he called you a coward, more than once.

RANDY. Hey, what is this?

JAMES. What?

RANDY. You need to interrogate the man? It's obvious he doesn't want to talk about it.

ARTHUR. It's no big deal.

RANDY. Why are you forcing him to talk about this?

JAMES. We're just having a conversation.

RANDY. Just a conversation —

JAMES. Arthur and I talk to each other. We've known each other a long time.

RANDY. Why don't you give people a break?

JAMES. What do you mean by that?

RANDY. You've always got to get in everybody's business.

JAMES. I do?

RANDY. "Stay in school, Franco." "Tell me why Ray Cockrot called you a coward— "

ARTHUR. — Klapprott—

RANDY. You're like a fuckin' after-school special. You hear yourself?

JAMES. Is that bad advice? "Stay in school," is that *wrong*?

RANDY. What is this, are you the captain of the starship now? Captain what's-his-fuck on *Deep Space Now*?

JAMES. *Nine*! *Deep Space Nine*, damn it!

RANDY. Who gives a fuck?!

JAMES. You say that shit on purpose!

RANDY. We can't get along unless you fix everybody, right, Captain?

JAMES. Hey, Randy.

RANDY. Arthur just wants to be left alone. He knows we care about him. We don't have to spell that out. I think he knows how we feel. So I think it's pretty clear he's not interested in us! That's clear! *(She storms out.)*

JAMES. Where did that come from? *(Arthur shrugs.)* This is my job. Solving problems is a part of the job. Settling disputes. I'm just taking care of my business.

ARTHUR. Right.

JAMES. I'm not trying to make myself more important than I am.

ARTHUR. I know. *(James sits, stews.)*

JAMES. I hate having people mad at me. *(James exits. Arthur calls into the kitchen.)*

ARTHUR. Franco, I blew it. I was almost there and I tightened up. If James hadn't come in. I would've pulled the trigger if James hadn't come in. *(Franco enters with another plate, another donut.)*

FRANCO. You just gotta wade in there, man. If you get knocked around, you get knocked around. No way to protect yourself.

ARTHUR. And how do you know this? You've been knocked around?

FRANCO. I can't complain.

ARTHUR. You can't?

FRANCO. I won't. Now try this please. *(Arthur tries the donut, makes a face: "pretty good.")* It's good?

ARTHUR. I think you nailed it.

FRANCO. Nailed it!

ARTHUR. That's a very good donut.

FRANCO. And that's from *my dough*, too. I made that donut from the ground up.

ARTHUR. That's right.

FRANCO. Look out now, I start crankin' out delicious dessert cakes and everyone's just gonna have to get the hell out the way.

ARTHUR. You're on the path to donut greatness. Which reminds me, I had a thought about your book.

FRANCO. What's that?

ARTHUR. I thought of someone we might get to look at your book.

FRANCO. Who?

ARTHUR. Look, this isn't anything, but — I see the look in your eye, and I'm telling you, this isn't anything.

FRANCO. What.

ARTHUR. My ex-wife's brother's ... partner. He wrote — used to write little restaurant notices for the *Reader.*

FRANCO. And?

ARTHUR. And nothing, that's all I got. A guy used to write restaurant notices, for a free paper. That's as close to a publisher as I can get you. If I can even track him down. But it's a place to start. *(Franco leaps in the air, screams, dances, pumps his fists.)* Okay, okay —

FRANCO. HELL yeah! Look out, Arthur P., 'cause here we come, baby, back from the dead! Ain't no stopping us now, man! Let me tell you how it's gonna be: This man is gonna read *America Will Be* and he'll set me up with the next man I need to talk to and *that* man's gonna put a check in my hand —

ARTHUR. — Right, yes, a big check —

FRANCO. — And they're gonna print my book and we'll put my book right here in a big display in the window that says "The Great American Novel."

ARTHUR. Very catchy, why not.

FRANCO. And meanwhile you and me are poppin' out the delicious dessert cakes and there's people out the door of this place and down the street, lined up to buy my book and eat our donuts and drink our coffee —

ARTHUR. Yeah, hey, fuck you, Starbucks!

FRANCO. And then wait till we get Poetry Night going—

ARTHUR. The Superior Donuts, uhh, Literary...

FRANCO. The Superior Donuts Literary Festival and Poetry Jam —

ARTHUR. "It ain't horse fat."

FRANCO. And we get a microphone and a little stage right over here —

ARTHUR. I can serve some specialty donuts—

FRANCO. And we'll get all the people from the neighborhood —

ARTHUR. — The Countee Cullen Cruller —

FRANCO. My mom and baby sister'll be right over here, eating their donuts and listening to me read from my book.

ARTHUR. You know I bet James could actually help me get a liquor license — ?

FRANCO. You can have a little glass of wine with your cop lady friend, right, taking it all in, the King and Queen of Uptown, and your daughter shows up, too, to take her place in the kingdom, all of us together, a real home filled with books and ideas and food and family. *(Silence.)*

ARTHUR. That's not going to happen.

FRANCO. Why not?

ARTHUR. It's not going to happen because that isn't what happens.

FRANCO. We'll make it happen.

ARTHUR. Life isn't just what you wish for.

FRANCO. You know what life is?

ARTHUR. Derailment.

FRANCO. You're wrong.

ARTHUR. I'm old.

FRANCO. Sometimes good things just happen.

ARTHUR. *I used to know a restaurant critic.*

FRANCO. Like you said, a place to start.

ARTHUR. Dreaming's dangerous.

FRANCO. Dangerous to who? To you?

ARTHUR. You're going to get crushed.

FRANCO. What are you so scared of?

ARTHUR. I'm not scared of anything.

FRANCO. Are you serious? You don't talk, you don't vote, you don't listen to music. Why do you bother to get outta bed in the morning? You can't even ask that old lady out on a date.

ARTHUR. That's got nothing to do with this —

FRANCO. You can't even talk about your own daughter.

ARTHUR. You're way outta line.

FRANCO. Right, if I mention her, I'm just an employee.

ARTHUR. You *are* just an employee.

FRANCO. And you're just a tight-ass boss.

ARTHUR. Because I know a fantasy when I hear one?

FRANCO. They ain't fantasies, goddamn it, they're possibilities! Don't you even believe in possibilities?

ARTHUR. This conversation is over.

FRANCO. See, you're even scared to fight with me. You just wait and see, old man. Wait and see what happens with this book. I'll show you. I'll prove it to you!

ARTHUR. *(Wheeling on Franco.)* You'll prove it to me? *You'll* prove it to *me?* Who the hell are you? Come in here with your chewed-up notebooks and your goddamn pipe dreams. Even if I find this joker, and even if I convince him to wade through your frickin' legal pads and even if he pats you on the head, that isn't your *ticket*. It's just another dead end. They're all dead ends. You don't want to do yourself a favor, do me one: Grow up. Stop acting like a fuckin' clown. *(Franco exits. Lights shift.)*

Magda and I had our problems. Usual stuff. I didn't talk. I didn't listen. We didn't have enough money and I didn't care. No big deal. Nothing insurmountable.

Something went sour.

Joni.

Our marriage became an arrangement. Magda and I became partners in a business and the business was Joni. A child is born, and a kiss becomes a handshake, and you no longer cast a shadow in your own house.

I didn't know you had to have hope to raise a kid. I didn't know you couldn't raise a kid without it.

Five years ago last summer, Magda and Joni packed up the car to drive to North Carolina, where Magda had found a job through some relatives, cleaning hotel rooms. I stood in the driveway of our house while Magda and Joni got into the station wagon. Joni stuck her head out of the window, tears streaming down her face. I told her I'd see her soon. She saw right through me. I said, "I'll prove it to you." That was the last time I saw my daughter. She was thirteen years old. *(Lights shift. Arthur dials the phone.)*

Hi, it's me, it's Arthur. Sorry for all the messages, but I'm … I'm just getting a little worried here. You didn't come in today and I guess that means you're not coming in today. Which is … I mean I don't care at this point, but I wish you'd at least call me and tell me you're not coming in. Because then we could … I don't know, I guess I'm feeling like … like we had that argument and maybe, I don't know, hello? I just heard a click. Is the click indicative of something? Okay, well. The number at the shop is, you know the number. *(He hangs up. Thinks. Takes Randy's card from behind the phone, studies it. Takes a deep breath, dials.)* Hi. Randy. It's Arthur. Mm, Arthur, from the donut shop. Superior Donuts. I, I think you said this is your cell phone. And hey, I was just thinking that … *(Lady enters.)* That's Lady. Lady just walked in. Man, it feels cold out there. Um. Where was I? I thought if you were up for it, you, we could …

LADY. Can I have a donut?

ARTHUR. What? Yeah, uh. Randy, sorry, I just, it's getting kind of busy here, so I guess I'll talk to you next time you come in. To the shop. Thank you. *(He hangs up.)* Hi, Lady.

LADY. Can I have a donut?

ARTHUR. Yeah, sure. *(She sits as he gets her a donut and coffee.)* Looks pretty nasty out there.

LADY. Yeah. And the weather ain't so great. *(Arthur looks out the window, scans the street.)*

ARTHUR. You've got kids, right, Lady?

LADY. What's that?

ARTHUR. You have kids, don't you?

LADY. Oh, sure. Two boys, two girls. One of 'em's still alive.

ARTHUR. You've outlived three of your kids?

LADY. Yeah.

ARTHUR. That's awful.

LADY. One of 'em got shot by the coppers in a gasoline station stick-up. One of 'em had a grabber, mowin' the yard. And one of 'em died in the crib with that disease. Where the spinal cord gets a mind of its own and decides it don't want to live trapped inside those little bones no more. You know what I'm talkin' about?

ARTHUR. I don't think so.

LADY. Your spinal cord gets it in its head to go free and slitherin' out into the world. That's what killed my little Venus. Her spinal cord got its own notions.

ARTHUR. Wow.

LADY. It happens. Happens to all of us, just not so extreme.

ARTHUR. It does?

LADY. The body don't work together. You know how they say the heart wants one thing but the brain wants something else?

ARTHUR. Yeah, sure.

LADY. The spine. It don't speak up for itself much. But when it does? Look out. Trumps the heart and brain every time. *(Arthur thinks about this.)*

ARTHUR. You've still got one kid.

LADY. Walter.

ARTHUR. What's he do?

LADY. He's a bum. *(Beat.)* No, he's okay.

ARTHUR. You and Walter … you on good terms? I mean you talk?

LADY. Not so much.

ARTHUR. Mm.

LADY. He's got a lot goin' on.

ARTHUR. Right.

LADY. You got kids?

ARTHUR. A daughter. One daughter.

LADY. Aw. That's nice. Girls are better.

ARTHUR. Better than boys?

LADY. Yeah, they're just better people. What's your girl's name?

ARTHUR. Joni.

LADY. Aw.

ARTHUR. Yeah, Joni.

LADY. And she's still alive?

ARTHUR. Yeah.

LADY. Good for you. You still got time. *(James enters, out of uniform.)*

JAMES. Arthur, I have to talk to you.

ARTHUR. Okay.

JAMES. Come over here.

ARTHUR. You want some coffee?

JAMES. No, that's okay. Just some water. *(Arthur pours water while James removes his coat, revealing a Captain Kirk costume.)*

LADY. Holy shit.

ARTHUR. Wow.

LADY. The spacemen have landed.

JAMES. I know, I know. Arthur, listen —

ARTHUR. You look great.

JAMES. Right, thanks. Sit down.

ARTHUR. Where are your ears?

JAMES. What?

ARTHUR. Randy said you wear ears.

JAMES. She doesn't know what she's talking about. I don't wear any damn ears.

ARTHUR. Yeah, 'cause that might look odd.

JAMES. Me and Crystal were at the convention when I got a call on my cell phone. Franco's mother called me.

ARTHUR. His mother.

JAMES. Franco's in the hospital.

ARTHUR. What's the matter?

JAMES. They've got him over at Masonic. I just came from there.

ARTHUR. What's the matter?

JAMES. He's been assaulted. It's pretty bad, Arthur.

ARTHUR. How bad.

JAMES. Someone cut off three of his fingers. *(James indicates the last three fingers of his right hand.)* These three fingers. *(Beat.)*

ARTHUR. What?

JAMES. Yeah.

ARTHUR. Well, is he ... what, is he going to be okay? I mean —

JAMES. He lost a lot of blood but he'll survive. They've got him on some serious painkillers, you know, and he's still in the ICU, still pretty out of it. So he can't have visitors yet, but in a day or so. *(A moment, as this sinks in.)* I'm sorry, Arthur. I know you like that kid.

ARTHUR. Who did it?

JAMES. He wouldn't tell me. But like I say he's not making a lot of sense. He never said anything to you, did he?

ARTHUR. What do you mean?

JAMES. You never saw him dealing with anyone, or — ?

ARTHUR. No.

JAMES. You sure.

ARTHUR. No, no, nothing.

JAMES. Okay. If you think of anything. I gotta run.

ARTHUR. Right.

JAMES. I mean anything, you call me, you understand?

ARTHUR. Yeah.

JAMES. Take it easy. *(As he goes.)* Night, Lady.

LADY. Live long and prosper.

JAMES. Oh, one more thing. What's the story on this book?

ARTHUR. Hm?

JAMES. You know anything about a book?

ARTHUR. What about it?

JAMES. About all he said in the hospital is, "They destroyed my book." You know what that means?

ARTHUR. No.

JAMES. Okay. I'll see you. *(James exits. Silence.)*

LADY. Who's this now?

ARTHUR. Franco. The young man who works here.

LADY. That's rough. They'll patch him up though. They can patch up most anything these days.

ARTHUR. Lady, I don't know what to do.

LADY. Sure you do. You know what to do.

ARTHUR. I do?

LADY. Sure you do.

ARTHUR. I don't want to do this. I'm scared.

LADY. What are you gonna do, run away?

ARTHUR. I can't.

LADY. That's right. Why not?

ARTHUR. That kid. Because of that kid.

LADY. Which kid are we talking about here? *(Arthur turns, looks at Lady.)* Got it now, champ? *(Lights shift. Nighttime. Arthur and Kevin.)*

KEVIN. Who the fuck *are* you? *(Beat.)* Does Luther know you? *(Beat.)* Didn't you ask to see Luther? *(Beat.)* Anything you can say to Luther you can say to me.

ARTHUR. Go get your boss.

KEVIN. You said something about some money.

ARTHUR. I didn't say anything to you. Now go run and get your boss.

KEVIN. You got a big mouth.

ARTHUR. Don't waste my time. *(Kevin stares at him, uncertain.)* Your boss wants his money, right? So go get your boss and I'll pay him his money. *(Beat.)* I'm not calling any cops, all right? Now I guess your boss is sitting in a car about a hundred feet from here, so go get him and bring him in here so I can pay him his money. *(Beat.)* Shoo. *(Kevin exits. Arthur crosses to the phone, dials. Into phone.)* They're here. *(He hangs up. He waits. He waits. Luther and Kevin enter.)*

LUTHER. Hi. Arthur?

ARTHUR. That's right. *(Luther extends his hand.)*

LUTHER. Luther Flynn. *(Arthur stares at him.)* All right, whatever. What's this about? I'm getting paid?

ARTHUR. Yeah.

LUTHER. Well. Terrific.

KEVIN. Sure.

LUTHER. That's just terrific.

ARTHUR. Wait here.

LUTHER. I wouldn't be surprised if you'd already dropped a dime on me. Which would be silly. No one has anything on me.

ARTHUR. I didn't call the cops. *(Arthur disappears into the kitchen, reenters with a large Kotex box. Luther and Kevin share a laugh.)*

KEVIN. The fuck.

ARTHUR. Count it.

LUTHER. I trust you.

ARTHUR. Count it. *(Arthur tosses the box to Luther. Luther tosses the box to Kevin. Kevin sits down, opens the box, takes out sheaves of bills, starts counting. Luther winces.)*

LUTHER. Can I have a glass of milk?

ARTHUR. No.

LUTHER. Franco told you how to find me? *(No response.)* How is he?

ARTHUR. He'll make it.

LUTHER. Was that ever a question?

ARTHUR. He lost a lot of blood.

LUTHER. That's awful. He's a good kid. I've known him a long time. He used to run some bets for me out at Hawthorne. Christ, he couldn't've been more than fourteen? Fifteen?

ARTHUR. Run bets?

LUTHER. You know, where you don't want to leave your seat. He takes your money and runs to the window, makes the bet for you. Gets a little tip and he can make some bets himself. He's always had the itch, Franco. His dad had it, too. Action junkies.

ARTHUR. He doesn't run bets anymore.

LUTHER. No, I know.

ARTHUR. He's a writer now.

LUTHER. Is that so?

ARTHUR. Yeah. He's written a book. A great book.

LUTHER. Really. God bless him. He's a sharp kid.

KEVIN. And he's got this donut thing working for him too. *(Luther and Kevin share a look. Kevin continues counting money.)*

ARTHUR. You don't know about his book?

LUTHER. Can't say I do. Wait a minute. You don't mean that pile of garbage he tried to sell us, all tied up with cords? No, see, I've read a few books, and they didn't look like that. *(Arthur and Luther stare at each other.)*

ARTHUR. He's twenty-one years old.

LUTHER. Old enough to know better.

ARTHUR. Right, 'cause you and me, we only made good decisions when we were twenty-one.

LUTHER. I never forced him to make a bet with me.

ARTHUR. You never stopped him either.

LUTHER. That's a gray area.

ARTHUR. Know who talks about gray areas? People who exploit them.

LUTHER. Where you from? You're Chicago, right?

ARTHUR. Jefferson Park.

LUTHER. North Side Polish. I knew it. Kevin, I told you, right?

ARTHUR. You're South Side.

LUTHER. Bridgeport. Originally.

ARTHUR. Now?

LUTHER. Right here. Historic Uptown.

KEVIN. *(Replacing money in box.)* It's all here, Luther.

LUTHER. Great. Well —

ARTHUR. Wait. How much is there?

KEVIN. It's all here.

ARTHUR. How much? What's the dollar amount?

KEVIN. Sixteen thousand.

ARTHUR. Is that the total amount of money you were owed?

LUTHER. What do you mean? Yes.

ARTHUR. There's no bullshit. No add-ons, no extras.

LUTHER. No.

ARTHUR. No more juice.

LUTHER. The debt is paid.

ARTHUR. Then you don't ever need to see Franco again. Right?
(Luther hesitates. Kevin urges him to the door.)

KEVIN. Let's go.

ARTHUR. Right?

LUTHER. Yeah, that's right.

ARTHUR. Good. Whatever else happens, you're leaving with that money. You've been paid.

LUTHER. Yeah, okay …

KEVIN. I feel like an asshole carrying this fucking Kotex box.

ARTHUR. You really gave him the business, didn't you?

LUTHER. How's that?

KEVIN. Come on, Luther —

ARTHUR. You humiliated that boy's body and you think you can justify that. But you can't justify destroying that kid's story.

LUTHER. The end justifies the means.

ARTHUR. Y'know, it doesn't. It really never does.

KEVIN. Fuck him. Let's get out of here.

ARTHUR. Hold on.

LUTHER. What?

ARTHUR. You can't go yet.

LUTHER. Why?

ARTHUR. We're not through.

LUTHER. We're not.

ARTHUR. No.

KEVIN. Yes we are.

LUTHER. What are we forgetting?

ARTHUR. I'm going to fight you.

LUTHER. Sorry?

ARTHUR. I'm going to fight you. And I'm going to win. I'm going to beat you up. *(Silence. Then Luther and Kevin laugh.)*

LUTHER. Good night. *(Again, Luther and Kevin move for the door. Arthur grabs Luther's arm and Luther effortlessly pushes Arthur away.)* We're all done here, okay? *(Again, they turn for the door, and again, Arthur grabs Luther's arm.)* Goddamn it — *(Luther shoves Arthur more forcefully. Arthur falls.)* Now cut the shit, old man. We're leaving here now. *(Arthur begins to stand.)* Stay down.

KEVIN. Don't get up, you piece of shit.

ARTHUR. No, not him. I want to fight you.

LUTHER. You don't have a choice. *(Max enters, wearing a track-suit.)* Who the fuck are you?

MAX. I'm the guy who make sure this douchebag stays away from Arthur.

LUTHER. This is ridiculous. Kevin. Deal with this. *(Kevin approaches Max.)*

MAX. And this is Kiril. *(Kiril, an enormous stone-faced Russian, enters. His hair is dyed white-blonde; he wears a tracksuit.)* And he is the guy who make sure this douchebag stays away from *me*.

LUTHER. What the fuck is going on?

MAX. *(In Russian.) Kiruysha, zakroi dver. Otpusti zhaluyzi.* [Kiril. Lock this place up. Close the shades.] *(Kiril follows his instructions.)*

LUTHER. Arthur, this doesn't make any sense. Now use your head, please. What if I'm carrying?

ARTHUR. If you got a gun, you better use it. *(Luther looks around, perplexed. Max, Kiril and Kevin stand by the door, watching.)*

KEVIN. I'll take the German.

LUTHER. You kidding? Look at him. It's Ivan Drago, for God's sake.

MAX. *(To Kiril.) Idiot, on dumaet mui nemtsui.* [This asshole's so stupid he thinks we're German.]

ARTHUR. No one else gets in this. Just you and me.

LUTHER. What if I decline?

ARTHUR. Then I'll beat you where you stand.

LUTHER. What's the point?

ARTHUR. You don't get away with hurting my friend.

LUTHER. All right. Fuck it. Christ. *(Luther, out of options, gets out of his coat, hat, etc. Arthur awkwardly assumes a boxer's stance.)* Look at the fucking Marquess of Queensberry over here.

KEVIN. Kick his ass, Luther.

The fight:

The fight is long. And painful. It is sweaty and bloody. The fighters display great ferocity.

The fight involves fisticuffs, grappling, wrestling and found objects. The fight contains gouging, biting, kicking.

Arthur and Luther speak very little during the fight. They swear, they grunt, they cry out in pain.

Max, Kiril and Kevin are for the most part silent.

The fight goes through phases.

The early phase of the fight is somewhat of a surprise for both men ... that they are in fact engaged in a fight, that they land blows, that they receive blows.

It is apparent in the early phase of the fight that Luther is the superior and more experienced fighter. He is also in better physical condition.

The middle phase also holds a surprise for both fighters in that their opponent shows tenacity and resilience.

This fight will not be easily decided.

By the endgame, both men are bloodied and sweaty, their bodies bent with exhaustion. But ultimately, Arthur prevails, not because of dexterity or muscle, but because of his strength of purpose ... and Luther's ulcer. And although Luther will readily recover, Arthur has genuinely hurt him.

The fight is over.

MAX. May I say one thing, please? We believe this is over. There should be no more effort to retaliation. Yes? Because you have friends, I am sure, and they are bad men, I know, but I also have friends, and they are Russian, and so they do not give a fuck.

LUTHER. *(To Kevin.)* Get me to a hospital ... *(Kevin assists Luther to the door.)*

MAX. Wait. *(Max points to the Kotex box on the counter.)* Do not forget your box of Kotex. *(Kevin grabs the box, and he and Luther exit. Arthur has pulled himself into a chair.)* Well, old boy. That is the goddamndest thing I ever saw. If I live to be a hundred, I will never forget the fight I see in Superior Donuts.

ARTHUR. I don't know ...

MAX. What?

ARTHUR. I don't know if it did any good.

MAX. Maybe not for you. But I sure got the charge. You beat the piss out of that big guinea.

ARTHUR. I think he's Irish.

MAX. I don't care if he is Eskimo, he think next time before he hurt someone. He stick his finger in wrong asshole. *(Arthur and Max look at each other ... and start laughing. Then Arthur collapses.)* Pomogi evo podnyat. Davai otvedyom v ofis, polozhim na divan. [Help me get him up. We'll take him next door and lay him down in the couch in my office.] *(Kiril picks Arthur up in his arms.)* Bozhe, kakoi tui silnoi. Tui sluishal shto italyashka skazal? Govoril tui pohoj na Dolpha Lundgrena v Rocky. [Christ, you're strong. Did you hear what that guinea said about you? He said you look like Dolph Lundgren in that *Rocky* movie.]

KIRIL. *Mne chasto eto govoryat.* [I get that a lot.]

MAX. *Pravda? A ya dumayu nichevo obshevo.* [Really? I don't see it.]

KIRIL. *A posle etova mogu poiti k svoei barmenshe?* [When we're done with this, can I go see my bartender?]

MAX. *Opyat eta barmensha! Ostav!* [Again with this bartender! Give it a rest!] *(Transition. Two weeks later. Snow falls heavily outside. Randy, in civilian clothes, hangs a "Welcome Back" banner. A Tupperware cake carrier sits on the counter. Lady enters.)*

RANDY. Hi, Lady.

LADY. Where's Arthur?

RANDY. He's gone to pick up Franco, from his mother's place. You want coffee?

LADY. Yes. *(Lady takes her seat at the counter as Randy pours her a cup of coffee.)* Who are you?

RANDY. Lady. You know me.

LADY. I do?

RANDY. Randy. Osteen. You've known me forever.

LADY. Oh.

RANDY. Are you drunk?

LADY. No.

RANDY. You're just not accustomed to seeing me out of uniform.

LADY. You're different.

RANDY. Yes.

LADY. Can I have a donut?

RANDY. Would you rather wait and have some cake?

LADY. No, I want a donut.

RANDY. Sure. We're having a little party.

LADY. We are?

RANDY. Not a party so much. Well, sure, why not, we're having a party.

LADY. What's the occasion?

RANDY. Franco's first time back at the shop. Franco's first time out of his mother's apartment.

LADY. That's the colored fella.

RANDY. Yes, that works here.

LADY. The one got cut up.

RANDY. *(Beat.)* Yes.

LADY. You never see the bad stuff coming. Just always comes up behind you and pow! Socks you behind the ear with a glove fulla marbles. Sets you back a few steps. *(Max enters, followed by Kiril. Max carries a half-drunk bottle of vodka. He is drunk, more jovial than usual; Kiril seems embarrassed, sheepish.)*

MAX. Hello, good people. I trust you have wonderful holiday time.

RANDY. Sure. You?

MAX. Very nice. Very nice indeed. This is my nephew, Kiril.

RANDY. Hello. *(Kiril nods.)*

MAX. Say hello to the good people.

KIRIL. *(Mumbling, quiet.)* Hello. *(Max whacks Kiril on the arm, too hard.)*

61

MAX. This is your country now, boy. You have to speak up!

KIRIL. Hello.

MAX. *(To Randy.)* He is shy. I believe you are having a party. Yes? *(No response.)* Delightful. I trust we do not interrupt. *(No response. Max opens the cake carrier.)* The cake looks wonderful. Did you bake that cake?

RANDY. I did.

MAX. I will be standing in line for a big piece, please. You will know me from my smile across from ear to ear. My oh my, it is a wonderful January day for a party, is it not? The world is white; the air is snap. How do you say this?

RANDY. I don't know what you're saying.

MAX. Don't you say this? "The air is snap."

RANDY. No, I don't say that.

MAX. You don't know what I am —

RANDY. Oh yeah, "there's a snap in the air."

MAX. There's a snap in the air?

RANDY. Yeah, I don't know anyone who says that.

MAX. Well, it is a wonderful day, with or without the snap. *(Arthur, James, and Franco enter. Arthur is bruised, cut. Franco wears a bandage on his right hand.)*

RANDY. There we are.

ARTHUR. Here we go. The place looks great.

MAX. The man of the hour! *(Franco nods, offers quiet greetings ...)*

ARTHUR. Take a seat.

RANDY. Can I get you something?

MAX. Yes, make yourself at home!

RANDY. What do you want? Do you want some coffee, or — ?

JAMES. Yeah, get yourself something —

RANDY. I bought some beer. Do you want a beer?

FRANCO. *(Quietly.)* No, I'm good. *(Franco moves to a chair, sits, his head down. Then silence. Max walks up to Franco, pulling Kiril behind him.)*

MAX. This is my oldest sister's oldest boy, Kiril Ivakin. Kiril, say hello to the man of the hour.

KIRIL. Hello. *(Kiril extends his hand. Franco looks at it. Max pulls Kiril away.)*

ARTHUR. Does the old place look the same to you?

JAMES. Looks kind of like a donut shop, don't it?

MAX. It looks better with you in it, young Franco!

JAMES. That's the truth.

RANDY. No, hey, there's been an improvement. Show him, Arthur. *(Arthur goes behind the counter, displays a small new boom box.)* How about that, huh?

ARTHUR. You wanted a radio. There you go.

JAMES. Before you know it, there's going to be a pool table in here.

MAX. Shop has gone sixty years without radio! No sound other than Arthur's beard, growing slowly! Now it gets radio with only one month left!

ARTHUR. I never knew I needed a radio and now that I've got one —

FRANCO. *(To Max.)* What's that mean?

MAX. What — ?

FRANCO. What's that mean, only one month left?

MAX. Sorry, I am drinking vodka and do not know anything.

ARTHUR. *(To Franco.)* I'll tell you later.

FRANCO. Tell me now.

ARTHUR. It's nothing.

FRANCO. What's that mean, only one month left? Month left till what?

ARTHUR. I sold the shop. *(Beat.)* I sold it. I needed the money. And it was time.

MAX. *(Bursting.)* I bought it. Finally. One hundred thirty thousand and now Superior Donuts belongs to me. It feels like a dream. My God, if my father could be here now and see me … *(To Arthur.)* You should have listen to me, my friend. You cannot live in the past. If we could change things. If life were different. This unhappy life. *(Max seems to notice for the first time that this is not being received in the spirit he intends it. Lady weeps.)* What's the matter? Turn on the radio. *(No one approaches the radio. Max turns on the radio, dances.)* Come on everyone, dance! It's my shop now and I say dance. *(He pulls Lady from her stool, twirls her to dance. She cries, but he laughs, props her up, dances with her.)* Lady, is a good day. Not a sad day. See? We are dancing at a happy party — *(Kiril gently tries to restrain Max.)*

KIRIL. *Dyadya Maxim, oni ne hotyat seichas tantsevat …* [Uncle Maxim, they don't want to dance right now.] *(Max breaks off the dance and slaps Kiril, yells at him. Lady is left alone, slumping, weeping.)*

MAX. Goddamn it, I told you to speak English! Do not hang down your head like a dog, mumbling in Russian. You are

63

American now! Speak up! *(Max sees that the party is spoiled.)* I am drunk now. My stomach is sick. Good day all. Good day. *(To Kiril.)* Let's go and eat some fried chicken. *(He swaggers out. Kiril starts to follow, then stops at the open door, thinks. He closes the door, crosses to Lady and gently assists her back to her seat. He returns to the door, nods graciously to the others …)*

KIRIL. Thank you. Thank you. *(… And exits. Silence.)*

RANDY. I'm going to cut this cake. Who wants some? Arthur?

ARTHUR. Yeah, it looks good.

RANDY. It is good.

ARTHUR. What kind of cake is it?

RANDY. Red velvet.

ARTHUR. That sounds good.

JAMES. I better get going too, actually. My wife's waiting for me. *(James grabs his coat, approaches Lady.)* Lady, you need a ride someplace? It's snowing outside.

LADY. I guess I gotta find someplace else to go.

JAMES. Where would you like to go?

LADY. If you're headed south, I'm going to a meeting at the Rec Room.

JAMES. What if I'm going north?

LADY. Then I'm going to Ole St. Andrew's Bar. *(James lays his hand on Franco's shoulder.)*

JAMES. You promised your mother you'd be home in a couple of hours, right? *(Franco nods.)* Arthur? You'll take care of him?

ARTHUR. I'll take care of him.

JAMES. All right. Take it easy, Franco. I'll see you around. *(To Randy.)* See you tomorrow, pardner. *(Lady looks pained and perhaps even a little panicked as she takes a final look at the shop. James escorts her out. Arthur and Randy share a private communication, eyes only.)*

RANDY. All right. I'm out of here. *(Randy grabs her coat, lays her hand on Franco's shoulder.)* Great to see you. *(She gives the "call me" signal to Arthur, who nods. She exits, leaving Arthur and Franco alone.)*

ARTHUR. Hey. I did it. I called her. We've had one lunch and one dinner. It's nice. No, not nice, it's great. Could be great. *(Silence.)* You want some of this cake? *(Arthur eats cake.)* I think they finally gave up trying to figure out who broke into the shop, Randy and James. I'm pretty sure it was Ray Klapprott, my old assistant. *(Silence.)* Ray supports the war. He's got a brother there and. I got in an argument with him about it. I don't know, I'd just gotten the news about Magda — that's my wife — and I was feeling ... Anyway, he took exception to my ... history. He got offended and quit. *(Silence.)* You don't know what I'm talking about, do you? Magda, or the war ... my history. My parents. Maybe I can tell you about myself. *(Silence.)* Look, don't take this hard, me selling the place. It's just a place, for Chrissake. I'm almost sixty years old and I've. I'm. I've run this place long enough. And I've got some money in the bank. For a change. Max and I agreed to give me the month. Just to make the, y'know, the transition. I'm going to see if I can sell off some of this stuff. The register's no good anymore, but someone'll buy that freezer. *(Silence.)* Now you're not talking to me? Is that the thing? I deserve a break, right? And I got paid for it. We ... both of us, we got helped.

FRANCO. I didn't ask for no handouts.

ARTHUR. I know that.

FRANCO. I'm gonna pay you back too, every penny of it.

ARTHUR. Okay.

FRANCO. Don't expect me to walk around kissin' your ass.

ARTHUR. I don't expect that.

FRANCO. Yeah, you better not.

ARTHUR. I also don't expect to be treated like an asshole. All right? I didn't just do it for you. *(Silence.)* All right, screw it ... *(Arthur takes his cake plate behind the counter, drops it, breaks it. Franco cries, quietly, holds his bandaged hand in front of him. Arthur turns to him.)* Franco. *(Franco refuses to look at him. Arthur takes a step toward him.)* Franco. Look at me. *(Franco does not. Arthur goes behind the counter, gets a notebook and pen, rejoins Franco at the table. Arthur opens the notebook, smooths out a blank page, and begins to write, speaking the words out loud as he does.)* "America ... Will ... Be." *(Franco looks up. Arthur and Franco look at each other. Blackout.)*

End of Play

65

PROPERTY LIST

Plastic grocery bags full of stuff
Wallet, money
Police notepad, pen
3 coffees in Starbucks cups
Cigarettes
Business card
Phone
Cookie tin, marijuana, rolling papers, lighter
Backpack containing marked-up notebooks, legal pads, typing
    paper, bound together with elastic bike cords
Apron
Broom and dustpan
Can of Coke
Small paper bags
Dollar bill
Counter rag
Joint
2 ten-dollar bills
Can of paint, paintbrush, mixing stick
Personal check
Money bag
Glass of milk
Plastic grocery bags with "book" inside
Donuts, plates
Coffee pot, coffee cup
Glass of water
Large Kotex box full of cash
Tupperware cake carrier, red velvet cake
Half-full bottle of vodka
Small boom box
Knife, cake plates
Notebook and pen

SOUND EFFECTS

Banging on door
Approaching rumble of bus, brakes, door opening, bus recedes

NEW PLAYS

★ **YELLOW FACE by David Henry Hwang.** Asian-American playwright DHH leads a protest against the casting of Jonathan Pryce as the Eurasian pimp in the original Broadway production of *Miss Saigon*, condemning the practice as "yellowface." The lines between truth and fiction blur with hilarious and moving results in this unreliable memoir. "A pungent play of ideas with a big heart." *–Variety.* "Fabulously inventive." *–The New Yorker.* [5M, 2W] ISBN: 978-0-8222-2301-6

★ **33 VARIATIONS by Moisés Kaufmann.** A mother coming to terms with her daughter. A composer coming to terms with his genius. And, even though they're separated by 200 years, these two people share an obsession that might, even just for a moment, make time stand still. "A compellingly original and thoroughly watchable play for today." *–Talkin' Broadway.* [4M, 4W] ISBN: 978-0-8222-2392-4

★ **BOOM by Peter Sinn Nachtrieb.** A grad student's online personal ad lures a mysterious journalism student to his subterranean research lab. But when a major catastrophic event strikes the planet, their date takes on evolutionary significance and the fate of humanity hangs in the balance. "Darkly funny dialogue." *–NY Times.* "Literate, coarse, thoughtful, sweet, scabrously inappropriate." *–Washington City Paper.* [1M, 2W] ISBN: 978-0-8222-2370-2

★ **LOVE, LOSS AND WHAT I WORE by Nora Ephron and Delia Ephron, based on the book by Ilene Beckerman.** A play of monologues and ensemble pieces about women, clothes and memory covering all the important subjects—mothers, prom dresses, mothers, buying bras, mothers, hating purses and why we only wear black. "Funny, compelling." *–NY Times.* "So funny and so powerful." *–WowOwow.com.* [5W] ISBN: 978-0-8222-2355-9

★ **CIRCLE MIRROR TRANSFORMATION by Annie Baker.** When four lost New Englanders enrolled in Marty's community center drama class experiment with harmless games, hearts are quietly torn apart, and tiny wars of epic proportions are waged and won. "Absorbing, unblinking and sharply funny." *–NY Times.* [2M, 3W] ISBN: 978-0-8222-2445-7

★ **BROKE-OLOGY by Nathan Louis Jackson.** The King family has weathered the hardships of life and survived with their love for each other intact. But when two brothers are called home to take care of their father, they find themselves strangely at odds. "Engaging dialogue." *–TheaterMania.com.* "Assured, bighearted." *–Time Out.* [3M, 1W] ISBN: 978-0-8222-2428-0

DRAMATISTS PLAY SERVICE, INC.
440 Park Avenue South, New York, NY 10016 212-683-8960 Fax 212-213-1539
postmaster@dramatists.com www.dramatists.com

NEW PLAYS

★ **A CIVIL WAR CHRISTMAS: AN AMERICAN MUSICAL CELEBRA-TION by Paula Vogel, music by Daryl Waters.** It's 1864, and Washington, D.C. is settling down to the coldest Christmas Eve in years. Intertwining many lives, this musical shows us that the gladness of one's heart is the best gift of all. "Boldly inventive theater, warm and affecting." –*Talkin' Broadway.* "Crisp strokes of dialogue." –*NY Times.* [12M, 5W] ISBN: 978-0-8222-2361-0

★ **SPEECH & DEBATE by Stephen Karam.** Three teenage misfits in Salem, Oregon discover they are linked by a sex scandal that's rocked their town. "Savvy comedy." –*Variety.* "Hilarious, cliché-free, and immensely entertaining." –*NY Times.* "A strong, rangy play." –*NY Newsday.* [2M, 2W] ISBN: 978-0-8222-2286-6

★ **DIVIDING THE ESTATE by Horton Foote.** Matriarch Stella Gordon is determined not to divide her 100-year-old Texas estate, despite her family's declining wealth and the looming financial crisis. But her three children have another plan. "Goes for laughs and succeeds." –*NY Daily News.* "The theatrical equivalent of a page-turner." –*Bloomberg.com.* [4M, 9W] ISBN: 978-0-8222-2398-6

★ **WHY TORTURE IS WRONG, AND THE PEOPLE WHO LOVE THEM by Christopher Durang.** Christopher Durang turns political humor upside down with this raucous and provocative satire about America's growing homeland "insecurity." "A smashing new play." –*NY Observer.* "You may laugh yourself silly." –*Bloomberg News.* [4M, 3W] ISBN: 978-0-8222-2401-3

★ **FIFTY WORDS by Michael Weller.** While their nine-year-old son is away for the night on his first sleepover, Adam and Jan have an evening alone together, beginning a suspenseful nightlong roller-coaster ride of revelation, rancor, passion and humor. "Mr. Weller is a bold and productive dramatist." –*NY Times.* [1M, 1W] ISBN: 978-0-8222-2348-1

★ **BECKY'S NEW CAR by Steven Dietz.** Becky Foster is caught in middle age, middle management and in a middling marriage—with no prospects for change on the horizon. Then one night a socially inept and grief-struck millionaire stumbles into the car dealership where Becky works. "Gently and consistently funny." –*Variety.* "Perfect blend of hilarious comedy and substantial weight." –*Broadway Hour.* [4M, 3W] ISBN: 978-0-8222-2393-1

DRAMATISTS PLAY SERVICE, INC.
440 Park Avenue South, New York, NY 10016 212-683-8960 Fax 212-213-1539
postmaster@dramatists.com www.dramatists.com

NEW PLAYS

★ **AT HOME AT THE ZOO by Edward Albee.** Edward Albee delves deeper into his play THE ZOO STORY by adding a first act, HOMELIFE, which precedes Peter's fateful meeting with Jerry on a park bench in Central Park. "An essential and heartening experience." *–NY Times.* "Darkly comic and thrilling." *–Time Out.* "Genuinely fascinating." *–Journal News.* [2M, 1W] ISBN: 978-0-8222-2317-7

★ **PASSING STRANGE book and lyrics by Stew, music by Stew and Heidi Rodewald, created in collaboration with Annie Dorsen.** A daring musical about a young bohemian that takes you from black middle-class America to Amsterdam, Berlin and beyond on a journey towards personal and artistic authenticity. "Fresh, exuberant, bracingly inventive, bitingly funny, and full of heart." *–NY Times.* "The freshest musical in town!" *–Wall Street Journal.* "Excellent songs and a vulnerable heart." *–Variety.* [4M, 3W] ISBN: 978-0-8222-2400-6

★ **REASONS TO BE PRETTY by Neil LaBute.** Greg really, truly adores his girlfriend, Steph. Unfortunately, he also thinks she has a few physical imperfections, and when he mentions them, all hell breaks loose. "Tight, tense and emotionally true." *–Time Magazine.* "Lively and compulsively watchable." *–The Record.* [2M, 2W] ISBN: 978-0-8222-2394-8

★ **OPUS by Michael Hollinger.** With only a few days to rehearse a grueling Beethoven masterpiece, a world-class string quartet struggles to prepare their highest-profile performance ever—a televised ceremony at the White House. "Intimate, intense and profoundly moving." *–Time Out.* "Worthy of scores of bravissimos." *–BroadwayWorld.com.* [4M, 1W] ISBN: 978-0-8222-2363-4

★ **BECKY SHAW by Gina Gionfriddo.** When an evening calculated to bring happiness takes a dark turn, crisis and comedy ensue in this wickedly funny play that asks what we owe the people we love and the strangers who land on our doorstep. "As engrossing as it is ferociously funny." *–NY Times.* "Gionfriddo is some kind of genius." *–Variety.* [2M, 3W] ISBN: 978-0-8222-2402-0

★ **KICKING A DEAD HORSE by Sam Shepard.** Hobart Struther's horse has just dropped dead. In an eighty-minute monologue, he discusses what path brought him here in the first place, the fate of his marriage, his career, politics and eventually the nature of the universe. "Deeply instinctual and intuitive." *–NY Times.* "The brilliance is in the infinite reverberations Shepard extracts from his simple metaphor." *–TheaterMania.* [1M, 1W] ISBN: 978-0-8222-2336-8

DRAMATISTS PLAY SERVICE, INC.
440 Park Avenue South, New York, NY 10016 212-683-8960 Fax 212-213-1539
postmaster@dramatists.com www.dramatists.com

NEW PLAYS

★ **AUGUST: OSAGE COUNTY by Tracy Letts.** WINNER OF THE 2008 PULITZER PRIZE AND TONY AWARD. When the large Weston family reunites after Dad disappears, their Oklahoma homestead explodes in a maelstrom of repressed truths and unsettling secrets. "Fiercely funny and bitingly sad." –*NY Times.* "Ferociously entertaining." –*Variety.* "A hugely ambitious, highly combustible saga." –*NY Daily News.* [6M, 7W] ISBN: 978-0-8222-2300-9

★ **RUINED by Lynn Nottage.** WINNER OF THE 2009 PULITZER PRIZE. Set in a small mining town in Democratic Republic of Congo, RUINED is a haunting, probing work about the resilience of the human spirit during times of war. "A full-immersion drama of shocking complexity and moral ambiguity." –*Variety.* "Sincere, passionate, courageous." –*Chicago Tribune.* [8M, 4W] ISBN: 978-0-8222-2390-0

★ **GOD OF CARNAGE by Yasmina Reza, translated by Christopher Hampton.** WINNER OF THE 2009 TONY AWARD. A playground altercation between ⬛⬛⬛⬛⬛⬛⬛⬛⬛⬛ Brooklyn parents, leaving the couples in tatters as t⬛⬛⬛⬛⬛⬛⬛⬛⬛⬛⬛⬛⬛⬛⬛⬛⬛⬛⬛⬛⬛⬛⬛ entertainment." ⬛⬛⬛⬛⬛⬛⬛⬛⬛⬛⬛⬛⬛⬛⬛⬛⬛ ⬛ure bile." –*Variety.*

★ **THE** ⬛⬛⬛⬛⬛⬛⬛⬛⬛⬛⬛⬛⬛⬛⬛⬛⬛⬛⬛⬛⬛ to Dublin to look ⬛⬛⬛⬛⬛⬛⬛⬛⬛⬛⬛⬛⬛⬛⬛⬛⬛⬛⬛⬛ and Nicky are hole⬛⬛⬛⬛⬛⬛⬛⬛⬛⬛⬛⬛⬛⬛⬛⬛⬛ the arrival of a stra⬛⬛⬛⬛⬛⬛⬛⬛⬛⬛⬛⬛⬛⬛⬛⬛⬛ "Dark and enthralling Christmas fable." –*NY Times.* "A timeless classic. –*Hollywood Reporter.* [5M] ISBN: 978-0-8222-2284-2

★ **THE NEW CENTURY by Paul Rudnick.** When the playwright is Paul Rudnick, expectations are geared for a play both hilarious and smart, and this provocative and outrageous comedy is no exception. "The one-liners fly like rockets." –*NY Times.* "The funniest playwright around." –*Journal News.* [2M, 3W] ISBN: 978-0-8222-2315-3

★ **SHIPWRECKED! AN ENTERTAINMENT—THE AMAZING ADVENTURES OF LOUIS DE ROUGEMONT (AS TOLD BY HIMSELF) by Donald Margulies.** The amazing story of bravery, survival and celebrity that left nineteenth-century England spellbound. Dare to be whisked away. "A deft, literate narrative." –*LA Times.* "Springs to life like a theatrical pop-up book." –*NY Times.* [2M, 1W] ISBN: 978-0-8222-2341-2

DRAMATISTS PLAY SERVICE, INC.
440 Park Avenue South, New York, NY 10016   212-683-8960   Fax 212-213-1539
postmaster@dramatists.com   www.dramatists.com